WEIRDOS, WINOS & DEFROCKED PRIESTS

LUDLOW PORCH

 Peachtree Publishers, Ltd.

Published by
PEACHTREE PUBLISHERS, LTD.
494 Armour Circle, N.E.
Atlanta, Georgia 30324

Manufactured in the United States of America

1st printing

Design by Paulette L. Lambert

Library of Congress Catalog Card Number 86-61545

ISBN 0-934601-05-4

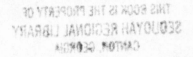

For Hank (The Prank) Morgan, who taught the rest of us what a microphone is for.

OTHER BOOKS BY LUDLOW PORCH

A View From the Porch

The Cornbread Chronicles

There's Nothing Neat About Seeing Your Feet

Can I Just Do It Till I Need Glasses?

WEIRDOS, WINOS &
DEFROCKED PRIESTS

Preface

SOMEONE ONCE SAID, "WE are what we eat."

If that bit of nonsense were true, I would be the largest trash compactor ever built, and most teen-agers in America would be a McDonalds drive-in window.

I prefer to think we are who we meet.

The people we come to know throughout our lives not only expose us to their personalities, but in one way or another they mold ours.

The process starts with our mothers and fathers, and it continues with grandparents, teachers, football coaches, preachers and friends. We pick up little bits from them all.

If our parents do their jobs early on, then we pick up good traits from the folks we pass on the road of life; if not, we might grow into adulthood thinking that a lifetime as a white slaver might be fulfilling.

I have been lucky to know many strange, outrageous, wonderful people. Some I was attracted to and some repelled me, but I can truthfully say that to one degree or another I have enjoyed them all.

This book is about these people — the good, the bad, and, in the case of Maynell Whitlock, the ugly.

Some of the characters are real, others are composites of several people. Most names have been changed to aid the defense in any lawsuit that might spring from the publication of this book.

One thought should be kept in mind as you meet the folks in these pages: We can learn something from every soul that we ever meet, even the weirdos, winos and defrocked priests.

Best Friends With the Bottle

IN THE PRESENT DAY vernacular, Sid would be called either an alcoholic or a substance abuser. He was certainly both of those, but he was more . . . much more. He was a drunk. A liquor-head. A wino. And a souse.

The point I'm trying to make here is that my friend Sid was bad to drink.

Sid would drink any alcoholic substance known to man, as well as a few known only to a select group of forensic scientists.

When he had money, he drank Scotch, bourbon, rum, rye and Irish whiskey. When money was tight and he wasn't (yet), he would drink anything from bay rum to Amoco unleaded. (He complained that Amoco regular gave him heartburn.)

Lest you feel sorry for Sid and his plight with the bottle, let me jump ahead in my story to reveal that Sid quit drinking when he was forty-five years old and is this day a respected member of society, and a wonderful husband and father, who for the past ten years has been living at the foot of the cross.

But in his drinking days, he was something else.

Whiskey had a strange effect on Sid. He was always a

nice man, but when he was drunk he loved most of mankind and *all* of womankind.

One night at the V.F.W., as Sid was leaving in his usual condition, he caught a man stealing his car. He didn't get upset or scream for the law. He merely said to the thief in a very kind voice, "Hey, Buddy, could you hold on a minute until I get my fishing tackle out of the trunk?"

The thief ran away and left Sid's car and fishing tackle intact.

Talking about it later, Sid said, "If I'd known how bad it was gonna scare that old boy to get caught, I would've let him took the dang fishing tackle."

When Sue Whaley announced that she was going to marry Sid, everybody in the county tried to talk her out of it. They all warned her of his "fallin' down drunk" lifestyle. She was assured by one and all that, with Sid in her life, all she had to look forward to was one drunken episode after another.

But when a nineteen-year-old girl is in love, no advice, no matter how well-intended, is going to be taken seriously.

Sue had the same reply for every advisor: "But I love him, and besides, he crossed his heart and hoped to die that if I would marry him, he'd never drink another drop."

She was partially right — Sid never drank a drop. He usually drank a fifth.

When everybody's pleas fell on Sue's deaf, lovelorn ears, they decided to work on Sid.

A group got together and appointed the Methodist preacher as their spokesman. It was his job to try and talk some sense into Sid. When the preacher finally found Sid sober enough to talk, he suggested that Sid join Alcoholics Anonymous.

Sid laughed and said, "Hell, Preacher, how can I join Alcoholics Anonymous? Everybody in the county knows who I am. Besides," he went on, "those people drink 'cause they have to. I just drink 'cause I like to be blind, stinkin', staggerin', fall-down drunk. It's not something I regard as a problem. It's more like a way of life.

"You're a preacher and I'm a drunk," Sid said. "You do good for folks, and I give 'em something to talk about. In my own way I'm a preacher too. The only difference is that you're preachin' against it and I'm preachin' for it. And you remember your sermons and I don't. You make your congregation feel good and I make every bootlegger in a thirty-mile circle feel good.

"Let's me and you have a little drink, Reverend, 'cause after a snort or two, everything I'm tellin' you is going to make perfectly good sense."

The preacher said, "My son, whiskey has never touched these lips."

Sid's eyes filled with tears, and he said in a soft, soothing voice that was full of love, "Preacher, that's the most pitiful thing I ever heard."

On Sid and Sue's wedding day, the church was full. Half the folks were there just to see if Sue would go through with it; the other half wanted to see if old Sid would show up sober.

Sid fooled half of them by showing up sober. After all, he said, this was a big day in his life and he wanted to remember at least part of it.

The ceremony went well. When the preacher got to the part that said, "If anyone here knows why this couple should not be joined in Holy Matrimony, let him speak now or forever hold his peace," you could hear a gnat scratch. Even the birds in the trees stopped chirping.

When the wedding was over, everybody hugged, and we all went outside the church to send the new couple off in style. We had Sid's Henry J. automobile all decorated with "Just Married" signs.

We never found out how old Sid behaved on the honeymoon. Sue was too loyal to talk about it and rumor was that Sid didn't remember much of it.

We do know, however, that when they returned, it was business as usual for Sid and his best friend, John Barleycorn.

I'm not sure Sid ever realized it, but over the years he was responsible for a good deal of the local entertainment. On Saturday at the barber shop, his exploits were always good for at least one story.

"Did you hear what old Sid did last Saturday?"

"Naw, what?"

"Well, he decided about eleven o'clock that night that he wanted a drink. Sue had hidden his car keys so he couldn't go after one. So that rascal took their riding lawn mower and rode it eight miles into town to the V.F.W. He had twelve or thirteen cocktails, a six-pack of Bud Light, and started home on that lawn mower.

"There he was goin' home on that dang thing, 3:30 in the morning, singing, 'I'm bound for the Promised Land' at the top of his lungs, drunker than a mixed breed possum and laughin' his head off.

"He was doin' real well and got within two blocks of his house before his luck ran out.

"Old Lady Rigsby's cat ran in front of that lawn mower and got all tangled up in the blade. That screamin' cat woke everybody in the subdivision up. When Old Lady Rigsby saw what Sid had done to her cat, she tried to beat him to death with a bedroom shoe. It must have been a sight to behold. It was kinda sad, though, Miss Rigsby havin' to go to a rest home and all."

The ladies of the town, however, did not regard Sid's exploits with the same cavalier attitude as did their husbands. Their conversations went more like this:

"Poor old Sue. I don't see how she puts up with it, livin' all these years with that out and out drunkard."

"Lawd, ain't that the honest truth. There ain't a place in town she can hold her head up. Poor thing."

"Say what ya'll will. I don't feel sorry for her. One fact you can't get around — divorce courts in this country are open five days a week."

"What about them poor babies? Ain't that pitiful, havin' a daddy that don't hardly ever draw a sober breath? Lawd God, they sure do need our prayers."

One summer Sid and three of his cronies decided to go to Carabelle, Florida, on a deep-sea fishing trip. Everybody knew that there would be a lot of deep-sea drinking and not a whole lot of deep-sea fishing.

They were on their way home driving up a two-lane blacktop road in south Georgia. Sid was behind the wheel. He was, as usual, possessed by demon rum and about three clicks out of focus.

The story goes that Sid was driving a little over a hundred miles an hour. Every time one of his passengers would urge him to slow down, Sid would laugh like a loon and say, "The police can't get me, 'cause I am the wind."

Suddenly, with his foot still on the floorboard, Sid topped a hill and saw, to his horror, a Georgia State Patrol car going in the same direction he was, but going about thirty miles an hour.

Everybody in the car knew they were about to be thrown into jail. Here they were drunk, and Sid, the drunkest of the lot, was driving. Not only that, but the fool was going over one hundred miles an hour.

Sid screamed to the top of his lungs, "Don't worry, boys, I am the wind." He slammed on the brakes and started to blow his horn in long, long beeps.

With tires sliding, Sid slid to within inches of the back of the police car, blowing his horn all the time.

The trooper pulled over on the shoulder of the road and stopped. Sid, horn still blowing, stopped behind him. One guy in the back seat moaned, "You fool, you're gonna get us all thrown *under* the jail."

Sid said, "Watch this. I am the wind."

He jumped out and sprinted to the side of the stopped police car.

In a high-pitched, excited voice, Sid yelled, "Thank God I was able to catch you, officer. I've been chasing you for ten miles. There's the worst wreck in history back there, and they need you at once."

The trooper said, "What?"

Sid screamed, "There's no time to waste. Women and children are hurt. In the name of God, man, you've got to get back there. Hurry, man! Hurry! There's not a second to lose!"

The officer said, "Thanks a lot. I'm on the way."

He turned his siren wide open, made a U-turn with tires smoking and within seconds was out of sight.

Drunk or sober, there were times when Sid showed flashes of genius.

He was primarily a city boy and pretty much ignorant to the mysteries of farm life. One day while having a drink or four with two of his farmer friends, Sid asked them why they had to castrate their bulls. "Sounds like an awful mean trick to play on any of God's creatures," he said.

They patiently explained to him that animals grow larger if they're castrated. Sid accepted this as the somewhat unnatural order of things and asked no more questions.

About a week later, Sid was home alone, drunker than usual. He was shaving with a straight razor and singing "When the Roll Is Called Up Yonder, I'll Be There."

He glanced out of the bathroom window and saw the billy goat that he had bought for his children walking around in his pen. Looking at the goat from the goat's south end, Sid couldn't help but notice how kind Mother Nature had been to his children's beloved billy goat. Despite this asset, however, the rest of him wasn't all that big.

Sid's mind, fogged as it was, raced back to the conversation he had with his two rural friends. Holding this thought, straight razor in hand, Sid staggered out the backdoor of his house and into the goat pen. He eased up behind old Billy and in one lightning move "did the deed."

The goat, of course, was instantly dead, and Sid was just as instantly sober. He knew what he had done, and he also knew that his family would be home soon.

He went to his toolshed, got a shovel, and within

minutes Mr. Billy Goat had received what passed in Sid's mind for a Christian burial.

When the "funeral" was over, Sid, still shaken by his awful experience, went back into the house and had a drink to calm his nerves. He was still sitting on the sofa when Sue and the children came home.

He called the whole family together and said, "I'm afraid I have some very, very bad news." With moist, blood-shot eyes, he continued, "Brace yourselves, because what I have to tell you is going to hurt. Children, the Lord has called our beloved billy goat home."

The children cried, Sue cried, and Sid cried loudest of all. They hugged and they cried, and they wept and they wailed.

Finally the thing that Sid had dreaded most of all happened. One of the children asked, "How did he die, Daddy?"

Sid paused in mid sob and said, "We're not exactly sure. I had the vet come over and he thinks he died from Hogan's disease."

Sue started to squall again. "Lord God, our poor old goat died from Hogan's disease. We never even knew he was sick and all the time he had Hogan's disease." She paused for a minute and said, "Sid, exactly what is Hogan's disease?"

Sid said, "I ain't exactly sure, but the vet said there's an awful lot of it goin' around. Said it strikes billy goats right in their prime."

Over the years I have heard many inspirational stories about how alcoholics managed once and for all to win their battles with booze.

The success stories range anywhere from a drunk's

being scared sober by stern, life-threatening words from his doctor to those fortunate ones able to get sober and stay sober when they find the Lord.

We have all heard about the wonderful work done by the men and women of Alcoholics Anonymous. If you've ever known a dedicated member of A.A., you know that they cut demon rum no slack, and their tireless work has saved countless lives and given their members a new lease on life.

I guess a search of the records would show that there are about as many ways to stay sober as there are to get drunk. But Sid's conversion was probably one of a kind.

Shortly before his forty-fifth birthday, he went on a bender and was missing for about six days. Like always, Sue was worried sick.

It was certainly not the first time Sid had been missing, but it never got any easier for the long-suffering and ever optimistic Sue.

Over the years she had developed a system that seemed to help her get through the worrying when Sid was on a toot.

The first day she ignored it and hoped it was just another of Sid's "nights out with the boys."

The second day she phoned around to Sid's friends to see if anyone had seen him.

The third day she checked with all the hospitals, and from the third day on she never left the telephone. She knew at that point that he was not hurt or sick and not in jail, and that soon the phone would ring and it would be old Sid, hung over, remorseful and anxious to have Sue come get him.

She always did. After all, she rationalized, he's a

hard-working carpenter, and how many other men could build a spare bedroom and new bath with no outside help.

It didn't bother Sue that Sid had been working on the new bedroom and bath for over three years and it was still only partially completed. Some parts had holes in them that you could throw a cat through.

She would make excuses to anyone who mentioned that the new bedroom and bath were practically outdoors.

She would day, "Sid's been so busy he just hasn't had a minute to devote to closing in those new rooms, but he'll finish it by and by."

On day six of Sid's last binge, he called Sue. He was drunk and crying, full of shame and self-pity and begging Sue to come and get him.

She picked him up outside a hotel in Atlanta. He was wearing the same clothes he had left home in. He had a six-day growth of beard, and all in all he looked like he could have been involved in an urban renewal project.

Sue was polite but stern. She knew that he was still half drunk, and that any lecture she gave him would not sink past the first layer of bourbon in his brain. However, she couldn't resist.

"Sidney, where have you been? I've been absolutely beside myself. Sidney, this must stop!"

Sid was crying, his large body racked with sobs.

"Oh, Sue! Please don't hate me. I'm sorry! Oh, I'm so sorry! If you just won't hate me this time, I'll never do it again."

"That's what you said the last ten times, Sidney."

"I know, I know, but those ten times I was lying. Now I'm telling the God's truth. If you'll just forgive me, it'll

10

never happen again. I swear it on my mother's grave."

"Sidney, your mother's not dead."

"I know, I know," Sid blubbered, "but someday she will be. Oh, Sue, don't hate me."

"I don't hate you, Sidney. Now, hush and go to sleep."

"I can't sleep, I'm too low-down and no account to sleep. I ain't fit to be in the same state with decent folks, let alone sleep. I ain't nothin' but gutter dirt, Sue, did you hear that? That's me, that's the white trash you married — gutter dirt in a double-knit suit."

Sue turned down the long driveway that led to their house. Sid was still sobbing.

Once inside, Sue said, "Sid, go take off those filthy clothes and take a shower. I'll fix you some breakfast."

"Sue, do you hate me?" Sid asked.

"Sid, right now I don't like you very much, but I don't hate you. Now, stop crying and go get your shower."

Sid headed off to the bathroom and Sue started breakfast. She was just starting to scramble the eggs when she heard a blood-stopping scream from the bathroom. Sid was screaming, "Sue, come quick! Please, come quick!"

In a near panic, Sue ran to the bathroom and snatched the door open. There stood Sid, his pants and underwear down around his ankles, his face the color of an Easter lily, and tears running down his unshaven face.

"Sid, Sid, what on earth is the matter?" she said.

Sid didn't speak for a moment, then he blubbered, "My, God, Sue, I've shit a possum."

Sue looked into the toilet, and sure enough there was a possum floating around. But she, unlike Sid, was sober enough to realize that the poor critter had wandered in through one of the holes in their bedroom wall and stumbled into Sid's toilet.

She instantly sized up the situation and conceived a plan. If she were quick enough to "seize the moment," permanent sobriety could be in sight for her beloved Sid.

Sid was still crying, "Don't just stand there, Sue, don't you understand? I've passed a live possum! Get me a drink, Sue, please get me a drink. Call somebody, Sue, don't just stand there. Do something."

"You go lay down and I'll call Doc Rivers," she said. "I'm sure he'll know what to do."

She reached old Doc Rivers on the second try, and in a whisper, so Sid could not hear, explained the situation.

She then went in the bedroom and said, "The doctor says he'll meet us at his office. Get dressed, Sid. Doc said there's not a second to lose."

Sid was only a little more composed as they went into the doctor's office. Doc Rivers listened and, to his credit, never cracked a smile.

When he'd heard the whole story, Doc sat back in his chair and said, "Sid, I'm gonna give it to you straight. Your body is in a state of advanced alcoholism. When that happens, there are two possibilities. Some folks get cirrhosis of the liver, and some folks pass possums. I'd say by what you just told me, Sid, that you are a possum passer."

Sid leaped to his feet. "Did you hear that, Sue? I'm a possum passer. God, help me, I'm a possum passer. Doc, you've got to help me. Doc, I can't go through life passin' possums. That ain't natural, Doc."

Doc Rivers, still fighting a smile, explained to Sid

that if he would stop drinking, he would never pass another possum.

It's been almost ten years since Sid had a drink. He is the president of the Rotary Club and teaches Sunday school. In short, Sid is a pillar of the community and the very soul of sobriety.

The only vestige remaining of his old life is the tiny tear you can see in the corner of his eye every time he passes a dead possum on the side of the road.

"Peachy Pie,"
The Irish Bulldog

LACY AND RUTH HAD been married twenty years but had never been blessed with any children. Like a lot of childless couples, they showered their love on animals.

They had a fish tank full of exotic fish, and each one had a name.

When Ruth fed them, she would say things like, "You've had enough, Norman, let Juanita have some food."

They also had a tomcat named Buster who spent his life looking for an empty lap to fill.

Their pride and joy and the light of their life, however, was their dog, Nicky.

I was never real sure what kind of dog Nicky was. He appeared to be a mixed breed of bulldog. Sometimes they would refer to him as a Boston bulldog and other times as a Boston terrier.

One thing was certain, however — all of Nicky's mixed parts were bulldog, from the tip of his mashed-in face to the end of his two-inch screw tail.

Once you found yourself in Nicky's company, you knew immediately that you were not dealing with Rin-Tin-Tin.

Nicky was a loving dog, but intelligence was not one of his long suits. His big trick was to sit and stare. He was also able to drool at will, but trick-wise, that was about it.

When you would throw Nicky's ball, he wouldn't have the foggiest idea what you wanted him to do, so he would go into his sit-and-stare trick.

When you tried to get his attention by calling his name, his ears didn't even twitch. The poor darlin' didn't know his name. That was not of great importance, however, since both Ruth and Lacy called him Peachy Pie.

The real tip-off to Nicky's low I.Q. came when he drank water out of his dish. If he saw his reflection, he would bolt and run full tilt to the other end of the house. Consequently, Nicky would drink water only if the lights were out.

None of this, however, made a bit of difference to Ruth and Lacy. They couldn't have loved him anymore if he could have done long division.

"Come see me, Peachy Pie. Mommie loves her Peachy Pie," Ruth would say.

"Does Peachy Pie want some cheese?" Lacy would ask.

If ever a dog knew love, it was Nicky.

When it came time for summer vacation, Ruth and Lacy decided on Myrtle Beach, South Carolina. As they made their plans, Lacy said, "What will we do with Nicky?"

"Why, we're going to take him," Ruth said. "You know I couldn't stand to leave my Peachy Pie for two whole weeks. Besides, he will just love the beach, I know he will."

So they drove to Myrtle Beach with Nicky on the back seat, sittin' and starin' all the way.

When they arrived, Ruth said, "Let's drive down the beach before we check into our hotel. You know I love to drive down the beach. Come on, Peachy Pie, get in the front seat so you can see the ocean. You're gonna love the ocean."

When Nicky saw the Atlantic Ocean for the first time, his ears went straight up. For the first time in that little dog's life, something had caught his interest.

The second the car was stopped, Nicky bounded through the open window. He hit the ground running wide-open toward the waves.

Ruth turned to Lacy and said, "I told you he'd like the beach. Look at that baby dog goin' to play in the water."

Nicky was jumping the waves and having the best time of his life.

Lacy said, "Boy, he loves it, don't he? Look at that little rascal swim."

Ruth hollered, "That's far enough, Nicky. Come on back, boy."

Nicky continued to jump waves, paddling like crazy.

"Come on, Peachy Pie. Come on back. It's time to go to the hotel," Lacy said. He was becoming more and more concerned. Nicky was now beyond the breakers and still swimming wide-open.

Lacy shouted, "Nicky, I'm not kiddin'! Get your ass out of that ocean."

When it was obvious that Nicky was out of earshot, Ruth and Lacy stood there and watched him swim out to sea. When he was just a dot on the horizon, Lacy said, "That's the dawgest thing I ever saw."

Ruth was in shock. She just stood there in wide-eyed

disbelief. Finally, in a flat, emotionless voice, she said, "Lacy, where do you reckon Peachy Pie was headin'?"

Lacy said, "Well, allowing for tides and the Gulf Stream, I figure his first landfall should be somewhere off the coast of Ireland. You reckon he's an Irish bulldog?"

Would You Buy A Car From Lindley?

HIS FULL NAME WAS Lindley M. Aaron, and there were two things that he was famous for. One, Lindley had the reddest hair of anyone who ever lived, and two, he was without a doubt America's, and perhaps the world's, biggest liar.

He was not your everyday, garden-variety liar. He was creative beyond any liar who lived before or since. Lindley took lying to new heights. If random lying were profitable, he would have been wealthy. If lying were bad for you, he would have been an invalid.

In the vernacular of the Old South, Lindley was such a liar that he had to get someone else to call his dogs for him.

He didn't seem to lie about important things. It was his random lying that made him famous.

One day the subject of bicycles came up in conversation. Lindley said, "These new-fangled, skinny, English-type bikes are okay, I guess, but you know, they just don't make 'em like they did when I was a boy. Good strong frames, balloon tires. Son of a gun, we used to have some fun on those old bikes.

"I'll never forget the races we used to have. We'd get

at the top of this long, long hill, about ten of us with our bikes.

"I reckon it must have been over a mile to the bottom of that hill. We'd all get ready and somebody would say, 'One for the money, two for the show, three to get ready and four to go.'

"We'd take off down that hill like two and nothin', peddlin' so fast you couldn't even see our feet. Why, one time, I remember looking down at my speed-ometer and I was going over eighty miles an hour.

"That's all right, I guess, but that's not the good part. The good part is I came in fourth in that dang race."

Lindley would use his natural lying ability to make himself an expert on any matter up for discussion.

There was a story in the paper once about a champion catfish skinner. Lindley said, "That ain't nothin'. Anybody can skin a catfish quick. That newspaper guy ought to talk to my Uncle Fred."

Somebody in the crowd said, "Was your Uncle Fred a catfish skinner?"

Lindley said, "Are you kiddin'? My Uncle Fred wouldn't waste his time skinnin' catfish. Why, my Uncle Fred was a world champion whale skinner. Yes, sir, he was somethin' to see. They'd drag that old dead whale up on the beach and someone would take out a stop watch and say, 'Go to it, Fred!' Uncle Fred would crank up his McCullogh lightweight chain saw and cut a groove slap around that whale. Then Uncle Fred would tie a length of rope around old Moby Dick's tail, and he'd tie the other end to the trailer hitch on his pick-up and drive away. When the slack went out of that rope, there was old Mr. Whale, nakeder than an empty R.C. bottle.

Would You Buy A Car From Lindley?

"Yes, sir," Lindley would say, "my Uncle Fred could flat skin a whale. Still holds the Olympic whale skinnin' record. Fifty-four seconds flat. That there's a record the Russians will be shootin' at for a long time."

When Lindley got out of high school, he drifted from job to job, never quite finding his own special niche in the mainstream of the work force.

His first job was as cashier at a self-service gas station. His only duties were to stay awake and take the customers' money.

Unfortunately, he was on the night shift, and since he couldn't stay awake, he was unable to take the customers' money.

He did all right with the honest customers. They would knock on the window and wake him up long enough to pay. His problem came when the local teen-agers found out what a sound sleeper Lindley was.

Every teen-aged boy within a forty-mile radius would coast into the station, fill his tank, and drive off while old Lindley smiled and snored away the hours.

His next job was as a door-to-door vacuum cleaner salesman. It was here that his lying got him in trouble.

No matter how hard he tried, he could not tell the truth, the whole truth and nothing but the truth about his product. Somewhere in the middle of the sales pitch the company had taught him, he would depart from the truth and his old habit would take control of his mouth, and he would launch into some of the biggest lies ever heard by modern housewife.

"Yes, ma'am, if you owned the famous Little Giant cleaner, it would absolutely change your life. This amazing little machine not only cleans carpets, drapes and upholstery, it has the strongest suction ever recorded by the U.S. Suction Testing Company in their home office at Aberdeen, Maryland.

"Yes, ma'am, in an actual sucking test supervised by the federal government, this machine sucked the cover off a Spalding golf ball.

"Yes, indeed, ma'am, this little modern miracle of the space age will not only clean, dust and wax your lovely home, but it makes, without a doubt, the most delicious grilled cheese sandwich you ever put in your mouth.

"Say you're not feeling well — tired, listless and suffering from arthritis, kidney failure and shortness of breath. Not to worry, ma'am. Relief is only seconds away. Just turn on the Little Giant cleaner, put two tablespoons of Vick's VapoRub in the input valve, and in seconds you'll feel better than a six-legged cat in a sand pile.

"A little-known fact, ma'am, is that Sylvester Stallone was nothing more than an out-of-work actor when he bought his Little Giant cleaner, and look at him today. He's handsome, well-respected and a multi-millionaire, and I guarantee you, ma'am, if my dear friend Sly were here today, he would tell you that he owes everything to this amazing little machine.

"Consider, if you will, Elizabeth Taylor, another satisfied customer. Before she bought our machine, she was not only ugly but spoke with a heavy Russian accent.

"Before owning our machine, Clint Eastwood was not only short, he was also a woman.

"I can assure you, madame, that this little machine will make a happier, more fulfilled life for you and your family. And I can also assure you that, beyond a shadow of a doubt, Jesus Christ, our Lord and Saviour, wants you to buy this dandy little vacuum cleaner. You can look it up in Deuteronomy."

It was at this point in Lindley's spiel that he was usually thrown out of the house along with his Little Giant vacuum cleaner.

Before long, Lindley started to worry about his financial future. He tried several other jobs, but steady employment seemed to elude him. Then fate stepped into the life of Lindley M. Aaron.

His old-maid aunt on his daddy's side died, and Lindley was named in the will. There was no money involved, but he inherited a ten-year-old, four-door DeSoto and a vacant lot on Highway 54.

Lindley considered this to be an omen. He said, "Hot dang, now I can be self-employed. I'm going to open a used-car lot. I own the lot and any fool can look at that DeSoto and tell it's used."

He sold the DeSoto and bought two more cars.

He had always been a shrewd trader, and that trait, combined with a tongue that had never been bound by anything approaching the truth, made Lindley a natural. Soon he had a lot full of used cars and a concrete block sales office.

He put a big sign out on the highway that boldly proclaimed, "Uncle Lindley, The Working Man's Friend."

He decided it was time to change his image, so he bought a cowboy hat, joined the church and started to call everybody "brother" or "sister."

He felt it would add to his image as an ultra-honest businessman if he quoted Bible verses to people as they haggled over prices. He could make almost anything sound like he had just plucked it from the pages of the Good Book.

Once when he was attempting to sell a poor black couple a delapidated old Chevrolet, he put his hand on the husband's shoulder and in his deepest voice said, "Brother, you know what the Book says — 'Woe unto the man who does not recognize the wonders of powerglide.'"

The man said, "Ya sah, Mister Uncle Lindley. I reckon it say that, awright, but fact is, suh, you askin' a might too much for that old car."

Lindley got a real pained look on his face and said, "That hurts, Brother. That really hurts. It's an awful thing to dedicate your life to serving mankind in general and the motoring public in particular, and then have one of your brothers in Christ accuse you of asking too much for a car that once belonged to Franklin Delano Roosevelt."

The customer said, "Dat car show nuff belonged to President Roosevelt?"

Lindley said, "If it were not so, I wouldn't have told you."

The would-be-customer's wife said, "That's all well and good, but we can't afford the down payment."

Lindley said, "Sister, let's not discuss anything as vulgar as money. Let's direct our attention to the happy hours that President Roosevelt and his beloved Eleanor spent in this darlin' little car. Let's think about the fact that it has only 94,000 miles on it, and most of those were put on driving from the White House to take the kids to school. Let's talk about the historic value of this car. Why, did you know that General Douglas McArthur once changed the oil in this car as a surprise birthday present for President Roosevelt?

"Did you know that one of them I-talian popes once rode to Sunday school in that very car?

"Brother and Sister, I don't see how you can even think about money when you're standing here on the threshold of owning this historic vehicle."

The wife said, "Just how much is the down payment?"

Lindley said, "Two-hundred dollars. Just two-hundred and you can drive this wonderful car off my lot today, and I'll tell the folks at the Smithsonian Institute they're too late. I'll tell them that I've already sold this magnificent machine to as fine a Christian couple as ever lived."

The wife said, "We don't have two-hundred dollars."

Never slowing down, Lindley said, "There you go, Sister, being vulgar again. I didn't mean two-hundred in cash. I meant all the cash you happened to have, and we'll make up the difference in your personal property. Just how much cash do you lovely people have?"

The husband said, "Twenty-seven dollars."

Lindley said, "See there, you have twenty-seven dollars. What a nice start. Now, do you have a TV set?"

"Yeah, suh."

Smiling Lindley said, "Good, good. I'll allow you thirty dollars on the TV set. See how easy this is?"

When the couple finally drove off in President Roosevelt's Chevrolet, Lindley had all their cash, the TV set, a Maytag wringer washing machine, two albums of Nat King Cole's greatest Christmas hits, and their oldest son's basketball.

There are probably no records kept of the ultimate fate of the world's chronic liars. I would guess that most of them are buried in unmarked graves. This was not, however, to be the lot of Lindley M. Aaron.

"Uncle Lindley, the Working Man's Friend" had at long last found his place in the sun. He would often say with great and obviously deep-felt pride, "Used cars are my life."

It was at this point in his business career that he decided to do some heavy-duty, big-league advertising.

He reasoned that if newspaper ads worked for the honest car dealers, they would work twice as well for him.

His first ad said, "Uncle Lindley, The Working Man's Friend. Your credit is good with Uncle Lindley. . . . Everybody rides. . . . We finance anybody — drunks, ex-cons, out-of-work druggies or wetbacks. Small down payment and proof of church membership is all you need at Uncle Lindley's."

The truth of the matter was that if you had the "small down payment," Uncle Lindley would waive the church membership requirement.

Uncle Lindley had a special formula for determining what the down payment was on any car. It was the actual value of the car plus ten percent. If, for example, you wanted a car that was worth five-hundred dollars, the down payment was $550.00. And the monthly payments were whatever you could be talked into by the very persuasive Lindley.

If you made the payments, the money was all gravy and Lindley was happy. If you missed a payment, he was even happier, because that meant that he could repossess the car and sell it again. When that happened, he would smile and say, "Praise the Lord. I must rise up and smote the ingrate debtor in his pocketbook."

Would You Buy A Car From Lindley?

When the debtor objected to losing his car, Lindley would say, "It's in the Book! The Lord hates a whoremonger and a loan defaulter."

The poor man would say, "But I ain't no whoremonger."

To which Lindley would reply, "And, Brother, when I leave here with my car, you will no longer be a loan defaulter. Praise the Lord, I've saved the poor wretch from the pits of a burning hell by repossessing this car and thereby cleansing him of the sin of bad debt. Praise the Lord."

Lindley's fortunes soared. He started to advertise on radio.

His commercials were an immediate success. He wrote his own jingles and they were sung to the tune of "On Wisconsin."

"Uncle Lindley, Uncle Lindley. Buy your car from him. He is honest. He is truthful and each car is a gem. Yeah, yeah, yeah!

"Uncle Lindley, Uncle Lindley, The working man's best friend. Buy your car from Uncle Lindley, the man who does not sin. Yeah, yeah, yeah!

"Uncle Lindley, Uncle Lindley, you can't go wrong. Buy a car from Uncle Lindley 'cause he wrote this song. Yeah, yeah, yeah!"

The customers flocked to Lindley's used car lot, which by now had grown to over ten acres of plastic and neon signs, as well as several hundred shiny used cars.

Lindley had six salesmen working for him, and all of them were required to wear cowboy hats that matched his.

As Lindley's business fortunes improved, his standing in the community went up as well. He joined the country club and the Rotary Club and the American Legion. He became a Deacon at the "Doublewide Church of Highway 54."

There was only one thing left for him to accomplish, one mountain left unclimbed in the now-full life of Lindley M. Aaron.

Lindley's chief ambition was to star in his very own television commercial and have it run on Ted Turner's SuperStation. He would fantasize about people in Utah and Lipham, West Virginia, hearing his commercials. He wanted not only to be rich, he wanted to be famous.

When his first TV commercial finally ran, the response was more than he had ever dared hope for. Not only was his lot filled with customers, but he had telephone calls from all over the country.

He even had a long-distance call from Ernest Angley praising him for his religious approach to selling used cars and asking for a donation to help feed starving children in Vermont. Lindley told the evangelist that his cash flow was a little tight, but he'd make him a great deal on a used jeepster.

Mr. Angley declined to buy the jeepster but promised to send Lindley an all-weather bookmark to use in his Bible.

One day Lindley got a call from Detroit. The man on the other end of the line told Lindley who he was and indicated that he had a great business deal for him. He wanted Lindley to meet him at the Atlanta airport to discuss the possibility of making him rich beyond his wildest dreams.

Lindley, doing his best Johnny Olsen impression, screamed into the phone, "COME ON DOWN!"

Would You Buy A Car From Lindley?

When Lindley hung up the phone, he was actually trembling with anticipation. "Just think, a huge auto company wants me to open a dealership. What else could it be?"

The days until the meeting dragged by, and on the appointed day our hero was right there waiting for the automobile executive to get off the plane.

They went to a nearby restaurant for lunch. They had a drink, then lunch, then another drink. The executive finally lit a cigar, leaned back in his chair and, after blowing smoke toward the ceiling, said, "Mr. Aaron, how would you like . . ."

At that point Lindley interrupted and said, "Call me Uncle Lindley."

The executive went on, "Mr. Aaron, how would you like to own your very own new car dealership?"

Lindley said, "Hot damn! A dream come true, my own dealership. I can't believe it. Thank you, Jesus! Thank you, God! Thank you, Ted Turner!"

The executive managed to calm Lindley enough to continue.

He said, "Mr. Aaron, my company is willing to let you in on a ground-floor opportunity. We're introducing a new car, not a new model, you understand, Mr. Lindley, but a new make of automobile. It's the first new make we have introduced in many years, and, Mr. Lindley, if you can raise enough money to buy a dealership, the Ford Motor Company would like you to be the nation's first Edsel dealer."

"Can I do it?" shouted Lindley. "You bet your Yankee ass, I can do it. I'll borrow on everything I own. I can just see it now — Uncle Lindley's Edsel. I'll make millions, maybe billions."

Lindley was standing now, speaking in a loud voice and waving his arms. "I'll be the most famous car dealer in America. No! No! In the world! I can see it now, me, Lindley M. Aaron, a guest on the Carson show. I know, I know, I'll sponsor the nightly news. I can hear it now. The news is brought to you by Uncle Lindley's Edsel . . . America's first and best Edsel dealership.

"Know what I'm going to do? I'll tell you what I'm going to do. I'm going to fire that liberal ass Dan Rather. I simply won't have him giving my news."

The car executive said, "Mr. Aaron. The first thing you've got to do is raise the money. Then and only then can you become rich and famous."

When lunch was over, Lindley put him on an airplane and headed straight for the bank. He borrowed money on everything he owned — business, home, life insurance, everything. Uncle Lindley went into hock right up to the brim of his cowboy hat.

Today there are no longer any Edsel dealerships and Dan Rather is still employed.

Lindley is still employed, too, and if you'd like to meet him, just call the Little Giant Vacuum Cleaner Company. Chances are he'll come right out to your house.

Cool Cat? Not With Pete Around

PETE HATED CATS. HE always had. He was proud of saying that he had never owned a cat and couldn't understand why anybody else would.

When Pete got out of the Navy after World War II, he moved to the Florida Keys and became a butcher.

His life was happy for almost twenty years. He, of course, didn't own a cat, and it was rare to even spot one in the sparsely populated Florida Keys.

Then, for no particular reason, Key Largo started to be overrun with stray cats. They were everywhere in groups of five or ten.

When Pete invited friends over for a cookout, the evening was almost always ruined by a pack of cats showing up to see what Pete was cooking. He threw rocks at them, screamed every cuss word ever heard at them. Once in a fit of angry frustration, he threw a plaster of Paris pink flamingo into a group of his unwelcomed trespassers.

Little by little, the cats were making Pete's life not worth living.

While nobody else in Key Largo could figure out where the cats were coming from, there was no doubt whatsoever in Pete's mind. He told anyone who would listen, "Ain't no doubt about it. Them damn cats are being brought in here from Miami."

"Ah, come on, Pete! Who would go to the trouble to drive a cat all the way from Miami to the Keys?"

"Don't take no Rhodes scholar to figure that out," Pete answered. "It's them damn Yankees and Jimmy Carter's Cubans doing it."

"They come down here with a car load of them howlin', screechin' cats and drop them off. Sure as hell, that's what they're doin'. Ought to send all them Cubans back to Port-Au-Prince and make every funny-talkin' one of 'em take two Yankees and three cats with 'em.

"I'll tell you what ought to be done," he continued. "The federal government ought to put a bounty on everyone of 'em and a bounty on the cats, too. Can't even sleep at night for all that howlin'. Can't go outside without trippin' over a dad-blamed cat."

The cats were not Pete's imagination. It was rare, indeed, when you went outside Pete's house without seeing at least six cats.

Pete finally decided it was time to take matters into his own hands.

It was bad enough to hate stray cats with such passion, but, because of their increasing numbers, he was starting to hate the world in general.

He hit on a plan that he thought was foolproof. He would become a vigilante. He would be the Charles Bronson of the Florida Keys.

He brought home a can of sardines from the store where he worked. He had his dinner, watched *Monday Night Football* and then went outside with his can of sardines.

He opened the back door of his old fishin' car, opened the sardines and put the can on the back floorboard of the car. He left the car door open and went back in the house.

Pete then opened a Pabst Blue Ribbon and sat down to watch the eleven o'clock news. When the news was over, Pete watched Johnny Carson's monologue. When they broke for the first commercial, he went outside and closed the door on his fishing car.

If you had been watching Pete, it wouldn't have looked like such a big deal. But Pete knew that the simple act of closing that car door was his first step toward ridding Key Largo of cats forever. Using the sardines as bait, Pete had filled his car with cats and now they were trapped.

The next morning he started to work in his fishin' car that was wall-to-wall cats. Every color, every size, cats in the front seat, cats in the back seat, cats everywhere.

To get from his home in Key Largo to where he worked in Tavernez, Pete had to drive across "Seven-Mile Bridge," so named because it is seven miles long and all of that seven miles is over water.

When he was about one-third of the way across, he started feeling for cats and throwing them out of the open window. They sailed right over the rail and down into the water.

Pete was having the time of his life. It never occurred to him that he was doing anything wrong. He preferred instead to think of himself as the Pied Piper of Key Largo.

Suddenly, traffic stopped, but Pete didn't mind. He thought this would be a good time to catch and dispose of the remaining cats. He was so busy that he didn't see the ragged old van with the spray-painted peace symbols stop behind him.

A young lady in a long, flowered dress and bandanna got out of the van and walked up to the driver's side of Pete's car and said in a loud voice, "Just what do you think you're doing, redneck?"

Pete said, "I'm throwing cats."

"You can't do that," she said.

"Lady, if you don't believe I can do this, I think you ought to check with them eighteen cats I done throwed out. If you'll take the time, you'll find that right this minute they are trying with all their heart to swim the Gulf of Mexico."

It was at this point that the driver of the van walked up. Shoulder-length hair, bare-footed, wearing cut-off jeans, and a T-shirt that said, "Only animals eat meat." He said, "What's the problem with you, old man?"

Pete answered, "The problem is that traffic is stopped on this bridge, I'm late for work, and I'm sitting here talkin' to two nasty folks that ain't had a bath since before Zsa Zsa Gabor was a virgin. That's the damn problem."

The long-haired man said, "My name is Cloud, and . . ." gesturing toward the woman, "this is my old lady, Kent State. We travel the world in the name of peace, love and brotherhood, and if you put your hand on one more kitty cat, we're going to tear out your large intestine with our bare hands."

Cloud looked very surprised when Pete hit him in the face with a tomcat, and Kent State looked even more surprised when Pete drove off and left her standing in the middle of Seven-Mile Bridge with the unconscious Cloud at her feet.

Cool Cat? Not With Pete Around

When Pete got to work, one of his co-workers said, "Well, Pete, what kind of a day are you having?"

Pete said, "So far it's been very, very productive. I've rid the world of two doves and eighteen cats."

Happiness Is A Best-selling Title

MY BOYHOOD FRIEND, LARDO Dupree, got interested in music when we were in high school. He saved the money he made from his paper route and bought a guitar.

Lardo was soon playing in talent shows and was starting to build a local reputation. His big chance finally came when he was seventeen. He was invited to New York to try out for *The Ted Mack Show.*

His mother worked around the clock to make him a costume, and it was a sight to behold. It was a black cowboy suit with about fifty thousand sequins sewn all over it, and across the back in big sequined letters with little musical notes all around it was "LARDO." It was a sight.

Lardo's daddy took a magic marker and wrote "Lardo Dupree" on his guitar in a fancy script. To top off the entire outfit, they bought Lardo a white cowboy hat and a pair of bright red high-heeled cowboy boots.

He was a sight — all 5′3″, 260 pounds of him.

You could tell at a glance that not only was he ready to conquer *The Ted Mack Original Amateur Hour,* he was ready to take New York by storm.

Unfortunately, network television never got to see Lardo or his outfit.

On the way to the TV station, Lardo was set upon by a group of ruffians who dragged him into a New York alley and beat him senseless. His guitar was broken, his white cowboy hat and red boots were stolen, and his cowboy suit was thrown into the Hudson River. Unfortunately, Lardo was wearing the cowboy suit at the time.

Lardo came home heavy-hearted and tried to pick up the pieces of his broken career. He even wrote a song about his experience. It was called "I Wish to Hell They'd Bomb Ol' Broadway." The song never caught on.

Lardo's experience in that New York alley had a profound effect on him. He still wanted to be in show business, but his taste for singin' and pickin' had been all but eliminated.

He decided that if he indeed had any future in show business, it would have to be as a songwriter. That way he could write his songs and let somebody else go to New York wearing sequins and be beaten up and thrown into the Hudson River.

To keep body and soul together, he took jobs in small country and western clubs. But Lardo soon realized that he didn't like the night life. So he took a job with a band that was traveling all over the Southeast playing country fairs. But the band broke up and Lardo got stranded in Tupelo, Mississippi, and had to wire his daddy for money to get home.

He came home and made his parents a promise that he would settle down. They made him swear that he would get a "real job" and give up show business forever.

They wanted him to join the First Baptist Church, become a Mason like his daddy, and then find a good Christian girl to settle down with. Lardo wanted to tell them what they wanted to hear, and he wanted to do all the things that would make them happy.

Underneath all his promises, however, he wondered if he could ever give up show business as long as he was a failure.

On the other hand, he was tired of the many disappointments he had experienced. Maybe they were right. Maybe he would be happier if he gave it all up.

He decided to give their way a shot. What the hell — what had he ever gotten out of show business? Just a lot of heartache and a wet cowboy suit.

He made a promise to his parents that he was home to stay and that they could quit worrying about him, 'cause from that day forward he was going to become a pillar of the community.

The next Sunday when Brother Warr gave the altar call at the church, old Lardo hit the center aisle. Everybody in the church was squallin'. They had decided years ago that Lardo was going to be a worthless, no-account guitar picker for the rest of his life and, Praise the Lord, there he was, shakin' hands and huggin' the preacher and accepting Jesus Christ as his personal Lord and Saviour.

The very next Sunday he was baptized. The preacher put him under four times — one extra to get all that show-business sin off him. Lardo was cleansed down to the bottom of his guitar-pickin' heart.

The next step on the ladder of respectability was a job. Lardo's daddy said, "What you gonna do about a job, son?"

"I'm just gonna watch the want ads and see what turns up," he said.

"Lardo, you got any clothes that you can wear on a job interview?"

"What's wrong with the clothes I'm wearing, Daddy?"

"Son, folks just don't go on a job interview wearing clothes that got sequins all over them, and besides, them britches ain't never fit right since you got baptized in 'em. I think they shrunk about three sizes. Can you breath all right in them pants, son?"

Lardo said, "Daddy, I've been in show business so long that I ain't got no civilian clothes. Just about everything I own has some kind of sequin flowers or musical notes on them."

Lardo's daddy said, "Well, I can't have you out here looking for a job in them funny clothes. We'll just make us a little trip down to Robert Hall and pick you up some decent clothes."

When they left the Robert Hall store, old Lardo looked just like a chubby Adolph Menjou.

It took Lardo about a week, but he finally found a job. He answered an ad in the paper, and after three weeks of training, Lardo became our town's first Fuller Brush man.

His mama and daddy couldn't have been any prouder if he had been elected pope.

It soon became evident to all of the single girls in town that not only was Lardo Dupree back to stay, but he was also one of the town's most eligible bachelors. I mean, what else could a girl want in a man?

There was old Lardo not only fresh baptized in the church, but rumor had it that he was in line to become deacon. When you combined that with the fact that he was a full-fledged Fuller Brush man and owned two Robert Hall suits (one blue and one brown), he was what the girls' mothers liked to refer to as "a catch."

Every Wednesday night you could hear all the mothers talking after prayer meeting.

"Why, did you hear that prayer that Lardo prayed tonight?"

"I do believe that was the sweetest thing I ever heard."

"And did you see that suit he was wearin'? I bet it cost fifty dollars if it cost a dime."

"Don't you know his mama is proud of him. Why, Lawde, any woman in town would be proud to have him as a son-in-law, him being a Fuller Brush man and all."

"Do you know what I heard? I heard that on his sample case he's got his initials right on the side."

"You don't mean it?"

"That's what I heard. Right on the side. A big L.D. plain as anything."

"Say what you want to, he's by far the best dresser in church."

"Word is he buys all his shirts at Gallant Belk. Not only that, but he sends all his shirts out to be washed."

It was inevitable. Lardo didn't stand a chance. Within six months he was engaged, and three months later he again hit the center aisle of the First Baptist Church. This time with Helen Winston on his arm. The whole ceremony took nine minutes and fifteen seconds. Lardo had married the daughter of the county school superintendent and, what was more important to his parents, had taken one more step on the road to total respectability.

To most people, Lardo appeared to be a happy man. Even his mama and daddy thought that their baby had at last settled down. Lardo and Helen had been married now for almost two years, and to the world it appeared that the conversion of Lardo Dupree was complete.

Then one night Helen missed Lardo. She looked all over the house. She finally found him sitting on a stump behind the smokehouse with his guitar trying to remember all the words to the immortal "There Stands the Glass," as sung by Webb Pierce.

Helen didn't think anything about it. She just said, "Lardo, what you doin' out here in the dark with that old guitar? Don't you know you're missin' *Peyton Place* on TV?"

Lardo didn't try to explain, he just said, "Comin', Helen."

Helen didn't even think anything was amiss when she found a copy of Roy Clark's Big Note Guitar Lessons that Lardo had ordered through the mail.

The next day Lardo came home wearing a pair of red cowboy boots.

Helen said, "Why, Sugar, it looks funny for a Fuller Brush man to be wearing red cowboy boots."

Lardo explained it away by saying, "Helen, it's the latest fashion. You ain't nobody unless you're wearin' cowboy boots. That Hollywood fellow started it all. You know who I'm talking about, the one in *Urban Cowboy*, that John Ravolta, or whatever his name is."

Nobody in town had any idea that Lardo was the most miserable man who ever sold Fuller Brushes while wearing red cowboy boots.

He was sick of selling door-to-door. He was sick of

Robert Hall and his damn suits. He was sick of his life in general. Deep down in his guts, he knew that he was born to be in show business, and it was an easy matter for him to despise anything or anybody that he thought was conspiring to change what he knew was his destiny.

Helen had set the clock radio to go off at 8:30. She reasoned that they were due at Sunday school at 10:00 and that would give them an hour and a half.

She was not surprised that Lardo was not sleeping beside her. Sometimes on Sunday morning he would get the paper and read it while he was drinking a cup of coffee.

She went right to her shower and did not notice the note on the sink until she was drying her hair. It was in an envelope that had her name on the outside.

The note said:

> You people are driving me crazy. I'm going to Nashville. I'll send for you, but I don't much care whether you come or not.
>
> Signed,
> Lardo
>
> P.S. Your mama ought to be in a cage.

When the folks in town found out that Lardo was missing, the reaction was wide and varied.

Preacher Warr said, "May God be with him."

His daddy-in-law said, "God wouldn't be caught in the same county with that white trash."

Lardo's mother-in-law said, "He ain't nothin' but gutter dirt. You wanna know where he is? I'll tell you where he is. He's laid up in a hotel with some scarlet woman."

Helen said, "But I love him."

Lardo's mother said, "Why, I can't understand. This isn't like my Lardo. I bet he's sick. Yes, sir! Truth be known, my Lardo has got magnesia, lost his memory. Dear God! My baby's got magnesia."

Lardo's daddy said, "In the name of God, woman. It ain't magnesia, it's amnesia. But that ain't what's wrong with that boy, Mama. You know he's my own flesh and blood and I love him just as much as I would if he had good sense, but there's something we must face, as unpleasant as it is. Our son, Lardo, was born a dodo. He has lived a dodo, and, God forgive him, in all likelihood he will die a dodo."

While all this was going on, our hero was on a Greyhound bus, wearing red cowboy boots, headed for Music City, U.S.A.

Once in Nashville, he took a furnished apartment. He unpacked and hung up all his old show-business clothes, sequins intact.

Lardo knew that in a matter of days, Nashville would be at his feet. His fantasies knew no bounds. He would have a monster hit record, then another, then another, sold-out concerts from coast to coast. The world's first billion-seller album.

He even thought about the title of the best-selling album. He spent hours trying to come up with the right one. Lardo knew if he was going to have a billion-seller album, the title was very important. His imagination ran wild. How about "Lardo Sings His Guts Out"? No, that was not sophisticated enough. How about "Lardo Sings His Ass Off"? No, that wouldn't do either. Then it came to him. He would call it "Lardo Live at the Great Pyramid." He could see it now. There he was standing on top of the Great Pyramid, one spotlight trained on him, far below 200,000 Egyptians, applauding, screaming and throwing their turbans in the air, chanting over and over, "Lardo, Lardo, Lardo."

He would make movies with Burt Reynolds, TV specials with Dolly Parton. He would open his own amusement park and call it "Lardo Land."

He would do the Carson Show. He would buy a house next door to Johnny Cash. It would be so big that you could hold a dove hunt indoors. He would have a huge swimming pool in the shape of a sequin.

Yes, sir, Lardo's fantasy knew no bounds. Unfortunately, his talent knew many bounds.

He haunted every place in Nashville that might listen to one of his songs. He was able to make ends meet by playing at small clubs at night and working at 7-11 in the daytime.

The first six months he was in Nashville he lived almost entirely on hope. He spent over a week's salary from the 7-11 to get a demo record made. He went to every radio station within fifty miles trying to get it played. Everybody told him the same thing — nice title but the song won't sell, and the way you do it leaves a lot to be desired.

On more than one occasion, Lardo thought about giving up and going home, but he knew deep down inside his chubby little heart that he would rather die a horrible death than to go home a failure for a second time.

He knew that's what they all expected, and what's more important, with the exception of his sainted mother, he knew that's what they all wanted.

His second six months were worse than the first. The hope he had lived on was gone, and one lonely morning Lardo was forced to face one inescapable fact: He was never going to make it in Nashville as a singer/songwriter. He was tired of walking the sidewalks. He was tired of the rejection and, most of all, he was tired of feeling like a failure.

The only thing Lardo wanted to do was to give up, but he wasn't sure how. He had already decided he couldn't go home, and he didn't know where to go in Nashville to surrender.

For days on end he pondered his lot in life, suffering the pain of rejection that had become synonymous with Nashville. Finally he decided there was only one way out. He reasoned that if he couldn't manage his life, he could sure manage his death. Lardo decided the solution to his problem was to kill himself.

Once the decision was made, the only thing left to decide was how the foul deed was to be done. He ruled out a gun because he didn't own one and considering the current shape of his finances, if he had a pistol, he wouldn't be able to afford a bullet.

Cutting his wrist was also out of the question. Lardo was squeamish by nature, and there was no way that he could take a razor blade and cut his wrist. The thought of dying didn't bother him much, but he found the thought of pain to be a definite turn-off.

He could crash his car into a bridge abutment. Only one problem here — he didn't own a car. And he knew it would be almost impossible to get a Nashville taxi driver to drive into a bridge abutment.

He thought about jumping in the river, but his experiences in the Hudson River had convinced him that he didn't want to kill himself by drowning.

There seemed to be only one option left open to him — he would hang himself. That was it, he was going to hold a necktie party, and he would be the guest of honor.

He was delighted that it was payday at the 7-11, 'cause he knew that if he were going to kill himself, it would take some money to do it right.

He went from the 7-11 to the hardware store and purchased twenty feet of very soft rope. He stopped by the whiskey store and bought a quart of Jack Daniels. Then he walked back to his room.

Once inside, he said to himself, "I've been in Nashville all these months and today is the first time anything seems to be going right."

He dressed in his best sequined outfit, pulled on his red cowboy boots and sat down to write a suicide note. Unfortunately, Lardo was no better at writing suicide notes than he was at writing songs.

The note said:

> To whom it may concern: By the time you read this, I will be pickin' and singin' with Jesus.
>
> Have a nice day,
Lardo.

He left the note on the table, walked outside and caught a cab.

The driver said, "Where to, cowboy?"

Lardo said, "Just take me out of town about twenty dollars worth."

The taxi was soon out of town and roaring through

the beautiful Tennessee countryside.

When they were well out into the country, Lardo said to the driver, "Anywhere along here will be all right."

He stood beside the road holding the sack containing the rope and the Jack Daniels and watched the taxi until it was out of sight.

He walked off across a big grassy field. All he needed to find was a private place with a tree and he was in business, or, in his case, out of business.

He walked for about ten minutes and finally came to the top of a hill.

A beautiful meadow lay at the bottom, and there was a small lake and, most importantly, a lot of trees that would be perfect for a hanging.

He walked around the lake until he found what he considered to be the perfect tree. He was so busy looking for a spot to die that he didn't even notice the old man fishing at one end of the lake. The old man had watched Lardo come down the hill and walk from tree to tree. He was watching Lardo's every move, but Lardo never even knew he was there.

Lardo sat down under the big shade tree and took the rope and the Jack Daniels out of the sack.

The old man watched in stony-faced silence.

Lardo opened the Jack Daniels, held the bottle up as if he was making a toast, and said to himself, "For once in my life, I'm going to get drunker than a four-eyed goat and never worry about a hangover."

He sat there for about twenty minutes drinking and staring into space.

When he felt that he had consumed enough courage, he stood up, put the top back on the bottle, and placed it carefully on the ground at the base of the tree.

He started to climb the tree and mumbled to himself, "I hope I'm not too drunk to climb this old tree and hang myself, 'cause if I don't it's going to ruin my whole day."

Even in his whiskey-logged brain, he was able to reason that if his rope was twenty feet long he needed to be at least thirty feet up in the tree to make this suicide a proper one.

He finally made it to a large limb that he judged was about thirty feet off the ground. To be sure, he lowered the rope, and sure enough, the end swung back and forth about ten feet from Mother Earth.

Lardo took great pains tying the rope to the limb.

Then he thought, I hope a songwriter finds my body. He could write a great song about me and perhaps I could be famous in death. It ain't much, but it's better than dying a 7-11 employee.

It was time. Lardo wanted to get this over with before he sobered up.

He sat very straight on the big limb, looked up briefly, shouted in a loud voice, "I'm comin', Jesus!" and hurled himself out of the top of that great tree.

It would have been one of the world's truly great suicides except for one thing: Lardo was so drunk that he had neglected to tie the rope around his neck.

While he was falling, he waited for that sudden snap that would start his journey to Glory, but of course it never came.

He hit the ground on his back with a loud thud that seemed to shake the entire meadow. Lying there with his eyes closed, he thought, Am I dead? If I am, it sure hurts like hell to die.

He opened his eyes and saw the old man standing

over him, staring down.

Lardo looked up at the old man for a long time. Finally the old man spoke. "Boy," he said, "you don't know nothing about killin' yourself, do ya?"

Lardo asked, "Are you Jesus?"

The old man said, "Naw, I'm Eugene. You want me to help you back up the tree?"

"No, I appreciate it but I guess I'm kinda out of the mood."

The old man said, "What's them shiny things all over the ground?"

"They're sequins," said Lardo. "I guess I jarred them off my suit when I hit the ground."

The old man said, "Can I help you up, Lardo?"

Surprised, Lardo said, "How did you know my name?"

"Saw it wrote on the back of your suit when you was climbing the tree. How come you dress so funny?"

"'Cause I'm in show business."

"You sure you don't want me to help you back up the tree?"

"No thanks. Maybe later," Lardo said.

The old man said, "I got a string of fish down in the lake that I'm fixin' to cook up. You'd be welcome to supper."

"Well, I did kind of work up an appetite climbing that tree, and Lord knows, my social calendar is clear. Yes, sir, I sure will have a bite with you, if you're sure it's no trouble."

"No trouble at all. Bring that bottle of Jack Daniels with you. It'll go mighty good with supper. If you want me to, I'll help you get your rope out of the tree after we eat."

"Naw," Lardo said, "I think I'll just leave it up there."

During supper, Lardo told the old man his story. He talked non-stop. He started with the first guitar lesson and told him every detail. He told about *The Ted Mack Show,* about his dip in the Hudson River, his marriage, his job.

He told about running away to Nashville and what a failure he had been. He poured out his heart about being too ashamed to go back home.

When he had finished, he said, "Eugene, you're older and wiser than me. Where did I go wrong?"

The old man took another pull on the Jack Daniels and said, "Well, it seems to me that your worst mistake was forgetting to tie that rope around your neck."

Lardo was shocked and his voice showed it.

"Eugene," he said, "I can't believe what you're sayin'. Do you really think my suicide was a good idea?"

The old man said, "Well, Lardo, I ain't knowed you long, and I ain't had a lot of time to study on it, but from what you told me, I think your suicide was a dandy little idea.

"Look at it this way, my boy — you got no choice. You can't stay in Nashville, 'cause you ain't got no talent, and you're too yellow to go back home and face the music. Yes, sir, you were right in the first place. If anybody would be better off dead, it's you, Lardo."

Lardo said, "I can't believe what I'm hearin'. People are supposed to talk you out of killin' yourself, not recommend it."

The old man said, "Lardo, you got to have more faith in your own judgment. You ain't much, Lardo, but when you're right, you're right. Now get up from there and go on up yonder and hang yourself. You take my word for it, it's the only way out."

Lardo was angry now. He shouted, "You're sick in the head, old man."

Eugene took another long pull on the bottle and said, "Let's examine the facts here. You're out in the middle of Gawd knows where, wearing funny clothes with them shiny things all over you, wearing red boots, jumpin' out of the top of trees trying to kill yourself, and you think I'm crazy! Face it, Lardo, you're a failure and a dumb ass to boot!"

"Failure, am I?" said Lardo. "I'll show you who's a failure. You know what I'm gonna do? I'm going back to Nashville and become a success in show business."

Lardo spun on his heels and started walking back up the hill toward the highway.

When he was out of earshot, the old man chuckled softly and said, "Atta boy, Lardo, you ain't never beat 'til you quit."

Lardo caught a ride back to Nashville, and for the first time in weeks he got a good night's sleep.

The next morning he was on the street bright and early.

He was on his way to his job at the 7-11, but he was not going to work. He was going to quit. He passed a sign that said "Pyramid Music Company." He stopped dead in his tracks. The logo on the sign had a man with a guitar standing on top of the Great Pyramid.

Lardo said, "It's a sign, it's a sign from Heaven. God wants me to go in and audition my songs for these wonderful people."

He went in, caught the elevator and got off on the second floor. Straight ahead was a wooden door with a glass inset. The inset also had the pyramid logo on it. Deep down in his heart old Lardo knew that going through that door would change his whole life.

He was surprised when he got inside. He had expected to see a giant lobby with row after row of mahogany doors leading to private offices and employees busily running around making people famous.

Instead, he found one room with a baldheaded man in a seersucker suit sitting behind a desk. The desk was full of papers and it looked like they had not been touched since Andrew Jackson left Nashville.

The baldheaded man said, "What can I do for you?"

Lardo said, "I'm a songwriter."

"I know that. Now what can I do for you?"

"How did you know I was a songwriter?" Lardo said.

Looking bored, the baldheaded man said, "The sequined musical notes on your shirt were my first clue, and not many brain surgeons carry guitar cases."

Lardo made his pitch, played two songs and asked the baldheaded man for his opinion.

The man sat back in his chair, took a long drag on a cigar and said, "Well, I'll tell you, my boy. I didn't like the song much, and you can't sing at all. Let me give you a little piece of show business advice. In Nashville, Tennessee, songwriters are a dime a dozen. As a matter of fact, most people in Nashville are here because they think they can write country-and-western songs. And you want to know something else? Most of them can. That is to say, once you come up with a title, any fool can write a song. Writing song titles and selling 'em to these yahoos is where the money is."

Lardo said, "Hold on a minute. Are you tellin' me that a man can make a living just writin' titles for songs?"

"Yes, sir," the baldheaded man replied. "And plenty of money if he happens to have the gift of title-writin'. Tell you what, son. Bring me some titles and I'll give you fifty dollars for every one I think is good enough to sell."

Lardo knew he could do it. He was up most of the night writing titles, and as they say, the rest is history.

Lardo now has his own song-title business, and some of the biggest names in country music buy their titles from Lardo.

His first big hit was one called "The Horse You Rode in On."

He also wrote "The McCullough Lightweight Blues."

A few of his bigger hits are "So's Yo' Mama," "If My Mule Looked Like You I'd Leave Him in the Barn," "I'd Marry My Truck, But It Ain't Legal," "Lookin' at You Makes Me Slobber," "I'd Marry Your Dog Just To Get in the Family," "Too Much Beer Makes My Mama Sweat," and, "My First Husband Was a Polish Joke."

The money and the hits kept on comin'.

Lardo even expanded outside of country music. He reasoned that he had never heard a song that was written for gays, and he knew that was a big market. So he went to work and came up with a whole catalogue of gay love songs. He wrote "Born To Walk Funny," "Moon Over Bruce," and, of course, his most famous title, "Pass the Talcum, Malcom, You're the Chap for Me."

Lardo sent for his family. They came to Nashville and, as they say in the fairy tales, "lived happily ever after."

Max Had a Way
With the Ladies

I TRULY DON'T KNOW how Mr. Webster would define a womanizer, 'cause I'm not sure how many hard-core womanizers he ever knew.

For better or worse, it has fallen my lot in life to know many big-time womanizers. I therefore consider myself somewhat of an unofficial expert on them.

While they are all different in many ways, true womanizers have much in common. First, they are all either married or engaged. Being single and unattached takes you out of the womanizer category, and the highest distinction you can hope for is to be a skirt-chaser.

True womanizers will allow nothing to stand in the way of their constant search for a woman of loose morals. The fact that being caught could result in divorce, disgrace, loss of children, loss of job, and high alimony and child-support payments not only does not deter them, it never enters their minds. Much less that there is anything immoral or dangerous about what they're doing. And even if it did, they wouldn't be able to stop. It's what they are. It's in their blood.

The very nature of his lifestyle dictates that a womanizer be inventive. He must learn how to lie with great creativity. He must learn to budget his time equally between his wife, his job and his woman chasing. Note, however, that he will never allow either his wife or his job to interfere with chasing women. The fact of the matter is that he will never allow *anything* to interfere with his nocturnal activities.

A true womanizer never quits, and no woman is safe from his advances. If he strikes out with the waitress pouring his morning coffee, he does not feel rejected. Far from it. He simply regards her as someone with not enough taste to appreciate what he has to offer. He will simply go on through the day making his move on strangers and co-workers alike.

It would not be accurate to say that womanizers do not love their wives. That's not the point. They just don't feel any challenge in taking their wives to bed. A true womanizer once told me that taking your own wife to bed is like striking out the pitcher.

My friend Max was a womanizer. He had all the tools to do it with a great deal of style. Max was in his forties, had steel gray hair, was a sharp dresser and drove a fancy car. He was a lawyer and a partner in a large, prosperous firm.

His wife knew that he had an eye for the ladies, and while she had never caught him at anything, she had come close on at least a dozen occasions.

She had told him many times that she would put up with a lot, but that if she ever caught him cheating on her, she'd spend the rest of her life taking everything he owned or ever hoped to own. Max was assured by this lovely lady that adultery was not something she would put up with, and he was further assured by her that if and when she could prove something on him, she would take great joy in seeing him broke and in the gutter.

This knowledge worried Max, but it never even slowed him down. Remember what I said: It wasn't what he did, it was what he was. For better or worse, divorce or gas chamber, Max was an Olympic-style womanizer, and nothing or nobody was ever going to change that.

When the American Bar Association held its annual convention in Miami Beach, Max took his wife. It was not that he *wanted* to take her, he simply had no choice. She found out that the wives of his law partners were going, and Max was trapped.

Max, seeing the hopelessness of the situation, decided to turn it into a P.R. coup. He said, "Why, certainly you're going, my darling. Do you think for one minute that I would go to Miami Beach without you? It just wouldn't be the same. Why, what would I do there all by myself? You know how miserable I am without you."

She smiled, but she knew better.

The second day in Miami, Max was sunning himself by the hotel pool. At least, that's what he appeared to be doing. But like all womanizers, he didn't have time for such wasteful pastimes. While he appeared to be sleeping, what he was actually doing was a little free-lance bikini shopping.

He knew his wife could join him at anytime, so he was just looking. Max was lustful, but he was not stupid. He had been at it for about thirty minutes when his wife came up. She was fully dressed and told Max she needed the American Express card because she was going downtown with some of the other wives to do some shopping.

It was like music to his ears. He knew his wife's shopping habits well, and he knew that once she hit the stores with a credit card she was good for at least four or five hours.

In Max's womanizing mind, he figured he could make love to half of Miami Beach's female population in four hours.

He walked her to the cab at the front of the hotel. It wasn't that Max was that considerate of his bride, he had simply learned from years of womanizing that you can't be too careful, and he wanted to make sure that she was gone before he started to cut his swath through the beach.

When the taxi containing his unsuspecting wife was out of sight, Max returned to the swimming pool. He had the waiter bring him a vodka tonic and settled back to see if he could locate a bikini that contained the pick of the litter.

It didn't take long before he saw a shapely young lady sitting by herself. She was wearing a bikini and reading a book. Max said to himself, "She looks so lonely. Perhaps I can bring some joy into both our lives."

He walked over and sat down in the pool chair beside her. He was ready with his opening line: "I just finished that book. I hope you enjoy it as much as I did."

She looked up and asked, "You just finished a book on quilting?"

He never missed a beat. "Yes. You see, I own a string of arts-and-crafts stores, and quilts are one of our biggest sellers."

The door had been kicked open, and now all he had

to do was walk through it. "Can I buy you a drink?" he asked.

"Sounds good," she said. They had the first drink, then another and then another. When the third drink had been finished, Max used the oldest line in the adulterer's handbook: "We can drink cheaper in my room."

It worked. In ninety seconds they were on the elevator. Max glanced at his watch. His wife had been gone for an hour. He had approximately three hours left.

Once inside the room, things moved pretty fast.

They were lying on the bed, both still in their swimsuits (a condition Max planned to change in the next three minutes). He was hugging and kissing his new-found roomie when suddenly he had this strange, strange feeling that someone was staring at him. He opened his eyes and there standing in the open doorway with an armful of packages was his wife. Her mouth was open in disbelief, but her eyes were narrowed slits. Max stared back at her as waves of panic and fear swept over him. She spoke first. She didn't actually speak—it was more like a bellow. "You dirty son of a _____."

Max was so scared that he could hardly breathe. He jumped to his feet, the blood drained from his face, and he screamed back the first thing that came to his mind. "It's not me. It's not me," he pleaded.

She turned and walked out of his life forever. He didn't see her for a year, and by that time she was a very wealthy woman. A judge had seen to that.

The entire affair didn't change Max's womanizing, however. He's still chasing women as much as ever. The only difference is that he doesn't chase them in a Cadillac anymore; he chases them now in a ten-year-old VW.

To be a successful womanizer, a man must become an accomplished liar.

Womanizers don't regard lying as sinful or even less than honorable. They regard it the same way a golfer regards his putter, i.e., if you're going to have desirable scores, you must get good at it.

It's not enough to lie with a straight face. A true womanizer knows that to be successful he must be able to look directly into the face of the mother of his children and tell her a lie of such magnitude that it would shock the demons residing in the deepest, darkest recesses of Hades.

He must be able to bring tears to her eyes as he explains why he is coming in at 3:00 A.M.

"It was awful," he says. "The car in front of me skidded out of control and slammed into the guard rail. By the time I pulled the poor guy from the flaming wreckage and got the tourniquet in place, there was no time to wait for the ambulance. Seconds could have meant the difference between the poor guy living or bleeding to death. I put him in my car and drove him to the hospital. I got him there in the nick of time.

"I decided to wait until his family arrived. After all, I couldn't leave the poor guy there all alone. It just didn't seem right.

"I was with his wife and mother in the waiting room when the doctor came in and said that he would live. They were so relieved and happy that they jumped up and down and hugged and kissed me. That's the reason I've got lipstick on my collar.

"There was some talk about putting me in for the mayor's Bravery Medal, but I said, 'Look, I just did what anybody else would have.' That's the reason I didn't give them my name or anything. I just don't want a big fuss made. I'm sorry, Honey, I didn't call you and tell you I'd be late. I was just so worried about that poor guy that I don't guess I was thinking straight.

"The whiskey on my breath? Oh, yeah, I forgot to tell you that this guy was pretty drunk, and I guess I picked up some of the aroma when I was giving him mouth-to-mouth."

The true womanizer also must be able to bring tears to *his* eyes, in feigned pain, anytime he thinks one of his outrageous lies is not being accepted by the little woman (notice I said *accepted,* not believed).

He must know her well enough to know how far he can go before his lie is too much for her to swallow.

No matter how late he comes home, he must have a carefully thought-out lie poised on the end of his tongue, ready for use at a moment's notice.

"Herbert! It's two o'clock in the morning. Where have you been?"

"I've just been out walking and thinking, trying to get my life in order. You know, Agnes, we've been married twenty-five years, and I've got to tell you, no man ever spent a happier twenty-five years.

"Yes sir, God truly blessed me, Agnes, when he sent you to me. Your love and understanding have made every day glow brighter than the previous one. No man ever had a better wife, and that's what bothers me, Agnes, and that's the reason I had to be alone to think things out. You see, Agnes, deep down inside me, I know that you're too good for me.

"I know that you could have married a better provider. Oh sure, I work hard, and I make a nice living, but I'm not sure that any man could ever give you what you deserve.

"You should have diamonds and rubies, servants and fancy cars. You're the best there ever was, Agnes, and I saw that very clearly as I walked alone tonight. I did something else too, Agnes. I decided that I was going to resolve to be a husband worthy of a queen like you. Starting now, Agnes, I'm going to be a more thoughtful, loving husband and try in some small way to be worthy of your love."

Now, I ask you, what woman could question any further after hearing a lie of that magnitude?

Which brings me to my friend Stu.

Stu was without a doubt the most talented womanizer the South, perhaps the world, has ever known.

He had all the resources necessary for successful womanizing. He was handsome. He drove a nice car. He made a good living and was such a talented liar that I.R.S. agents believed him.

In Stu's single days, he found it almost impossible to have a passing relationship with a woman. Every woman he dated almost immediately became the love of his life. He would pledge his undying love and devotion to her and vow that the flame of his love for her would burn brightly until the end of time.

That usually meant for about thirty days or until he met the next "love of his life," whichever came first.

He was therefore usually juggling about three women at any one time. While he was out with one of them, he was busy making up lies to tell the other two.

His standard M.O. was to always tell them exactly

what they wanted to hear and to paint a picture so rosy that any woman would melt at the very thought of a future with Stu.

His favorite lie was, "Sweetheart, you know how much I love you, and you know that I would rather be with you for five minutes than to be with all the angels of Heaven for an eternity.

"Let me tell you what we're going to do just as soon as the rush is over down at the office. We're going to the mountains, just the two of us, and spend a quiet two weeks alone in a little vine-covered cottage.

"We'll take long walks in the woods in the daytime and sit in front of the fireplace at night. Yes, sir, that's what we're going to do, just as soon as the rush is over down at the office."

In nine out of ten cases, the young lady in question was pacified, and Stu was free to go on with his womanizing ways.

Stu became so famous for painting pretty pictures of things to be that he picked up the nickname "Sky Blue Stu."

After many years of holding auditions, Stu finally found "Miss Right." He told anyone who would listen that this young lady was the one he wanted to walk hand-in-hand through life with.

He asked her to marry him. She said yes. He promised her the moon and the stars, but, most importantly, he promised that she was the only woman he could ever love and that he would remain true to her until the end of time.

They planned a June wedding, and Stu did not see another woman for about four days. (This was a record for his fidelity.)

On the fourth day of his fast, he received a phone call from one of his many old flames. He promptly forgot all about his fianceé and invited his old flame by his apartment for some wine and God-only-knows what else.

When she arrived, Stu had the stereo playing softly, the wine chilled and the bed turned back.

In less than forty-five minutes he had coaxed her into the bedroom, and they were stretched out across the bed with only their underwear on.

There was a knock on the front door, and Stu told his nearly naked visitor, "Be quiet. Maybe they'll go away." No such luck. There was another knock, then another, then came the thing that all womanizers fear most—the voice of the fianceé.

"Stu, open up. Let me in."

"Don't make a sound," Stu urged. "In the name of heaven, don't make a sound."

The voice at the door continued. "Stu, it's me. Open the door. Stu, it's me."

Stu was in a near panic when finally the voice and the knocking stopped. He was safe; she was gone. By the time she got to a phone to call him, he would have had time to create one of his famous lies.

The next sound he heard was enough to knock a fence post loose.

She had left the front door, walked around the apartment and was walking toward the outside bedroom door. The door was only about two feet from the bed, and Stu remembered to his horror that it was unlocked.

He dived across the bed and grabbed the doorknob about the same time his true love opened the door. Stu pushed it closed; she pulled it open; Stu pushed it closed.

"Stu, is that you?" she said.

"Yes," Stu shouted. "Don't open the door. I'm not dressed."

"Oh, don't be silly, Stu. Stop pushing on that door and let me in."

"I can't," mumbled Stu, "I'm asleep. Go on home. I'll call you later."

Now she was mad and beginning to see the light. "Don't bother to call me later," she shouted, "As a matter of fact, don't ever bother to call me again." She turned and stomped off toward her car.

Stu fell back into the bed in a nervous sweat. What was he going to do now? What could he tell her to explain? He was so nervous and upset that he had completely forgotten the half-nude old flame lying beside him in the bed.

"Who was that?" the old flame asked coldly.

"Oh, nobody important. Just a friend."

While the old flame was dressing, Stu's mind was racing. What could he tell his fianceé? The thought of losing her was almost more than his lying, cheating, worthless heart could bear.

He tried praying. He said, "Dear Lord, please help me think of a lie. I can't do it by myself. God, please help me think of a lie so big and so foolproof that she'll buy it hook, line and sinker."

Since it was the first time the Lord had heard from Stu in about fifteen years, I think it is safe to assume that he chose not to be involved in Stu's womanizing.

Stu walked the floor. He had more wine and just when he thought his world was coming to an end, it hit him. Even in his near panic, it came to him. His years of experience in cheating and lying finally paid off.

Stu, at that moment, came up with the perfect lie.

He calmly walked to the phone, picked up the receiver and dialed the number of his fianceé.

She answered, with a cold, flat hello.

"Hi, Sweetheart, it's me," he said.

With ice dripping from every syllable, she said, "I know who it is."

His next line had to be just right and he knew it.

"Were you over here a few minutes ago?" he asked. Before she could answer, he went on.

"You know, I was taking a nap earlier this afternoon and I had the strangest dream. I dreamed that there was a mad dog outside my apartment and it was trying to get in to bite me. It was a really strange dream, because my neighbors kept calling my name to get me to come out so the dog could bite me.

"Then the strangest part of all, I dreamed that my neighbors got you to come over and help them by pulling on the bedroom door to open it and let the dog in to bite me."

He paused for the first time to see what her reaction would be. The ice and anger faded from her voice and she said, "You know, that explains everything." Then she told him her story.

When she had finished, a very relieved Stu said, "Yes, sir, nightmares are sure strange things." Then, anxious to change the subject, he said, "Where would you like to go for dinner tonight, my pet?"

"Anywhere you say, darling," she purred. "Anywhere you say."

My friend Clay was probably one the most active womanizers ever.

He decided early in life that he would devote his every waking thought to the pursuit of the fairer sex.

He was somewhat like a compulsive gambler. It wasn't the conquest that he loved; it was the challenge of the pursuit.

Clay was a real estate agent and therefore had a built-in excuse to get out of the house almost any time. I'm convinced to this day that had he spent as much time selling real estate as he did womanizing, he would be a rich man today.

He would create little games to play.

Like most real estate folks, Clay had an answering service. He discovered one day that the answering service had seven operators.

This represented a challenge to Clay. He made a vow not to rest until he had bedded all seven.

He was not particularly attracted to any of them, but that was not important to Clay. What was important was that, like Mt. Everest, they were there.

In less than ninety days, the score was six down and one to go.

Clay had used every womanizing trick he knew, but number seven still eluded him. Oh, she was friendly enough and even dated him several times, but every time he made his big move, she would just smile and say, "Look, Clay, I'm never going to bed with you. Besides, I've known your type before. You're a scorekeeper, and I don't go to bed with scorekeepers."

Clay was finally able to talk her into going to Las Vegas with him. It wasn't easy, but the lure of the bright lights and the shows were too much for her.

Clay, of course, told his wife that he was going to Vegas for a seminar.

The third day in Vegas, Clay's luck was starting to change. Good old number seven was starting to thaw.

Clay even got her to agree to come to his room after the Vic Damone show. She had promised him that tonight would be the night.

Clay was so looking forward to his sexual rendezvous with her that he had completely forgotten that it was his wedding anniversary.

Back home, however, his wife had remembered. She was talking to her next-door neighbor. "My poor Clay, so far away from home and working so hard. And he is going to be all alone on our tenth wedding anniversary.

"I could cry. This will be the first anniversary we have ever been apart."

The neighbor said, "Why don't you fly to Vegas and surprise him on your anniversary?"

Clay's wife smiled. "Do you suppose I could? It would be so wonderful to be together, and can you just see the look on Clay's face when he sees me? I'll do it. Yes, sir, I'll do it."

Late the next afternoon, she flew to Vegas, caught a cab and went to Clay's hotel. She kept thinking, Boy, is he going to be surprised.

He was in room 701. She glared at herself in the hall mirror, fixed her lipstick, made sure her hair was just right. Then she knocked on the door.

Clay opened the door. He was wearing only his pants, no shirt, no shoes, and directly behind him, sitting in a king-sized bed, sipping champagne, was good old number seven.

Clay couldn't believe his eyes. His wife's mouth was wide open in the international look of disbelief.

Seconds passed as Clay's mind raced. Finally, Clay spoke. "Sugar," he said, "are you going to believe your eyes or what I'm about to tell you?"

Before he could say anything else, his wife stomped off down the hall.

He plopped down in a chair and buried his head in his hands. Number seven spoke. "Who in the name of God was that?"

"My wife," he replied.

"Your wife!" she screamed. "Your wife? You never told me you were married."

"Oh, don't be childish," Clay said. "You know as well as I do that all men are married."

Clay went home, and through some miracle he was able to lie his way back into his wife's good graces.

He met some of his fellow womanizers at a bar the next night and they were, of course, full of questions about his Vegas trip. But old Clay would only smile and say, "Six out of seven ain't bad."

Pardon Me While
I Turn Weird

SOMETIMES THE WEIRDOS WHO pass through your lives are gone so quickly that we never even learn their names. If, however, they are wild enough, no matter how brief our association, the memory of them can stay with us for a lifetime.

I was driving my car in downtown Birmingham, Alabama, several years ago. It was a beautiful spring day and there was not a cloud in the sky.

I noticed that the car in front of me had its windshield wipers on. I followed the fellow about ten blocks, wondering all the way why anybody would have on their wipers on such a beautiful day.

He stopped at a red light and I pulled up beside him. His wipers were still wide-open — ker-plop, ker-plop.

I kept my eyes straight ahead. After all, I didn't want him to think I was staring at him. Just before the light turned green, he shouted to me, "Hey, buddy!"

I turned and said, "You talkin' to me?"

"Yeah," he said. "Your wipers ain't on."

When the light changed he drove away while I sat there laughing like a loon.

Once a police officer stopped a man for speeding. The policeman walked up to the car and in his usual stern policeman's voice said, "Can I see your driver's license?"

With no hesitation the slightly inebriated driver said, "Can I shoot your gun?"

I dialed the telephone once and a very cheerful male voice answered, "Joy Motors Used-Car Lot."

I said, "Please excuse me, I've dialed the wrong number."

The voice came right back. "That's perfectly all right, buddy. How about selling you a used car?"

I didn't need a used car, but I started to buy one from him anyway.

About ten years ago, while doing my radio talk show, I introduced my topic for the day. It was one I knew would spur some good comments and get some good conversation going. My topic was, "What is the government doing for you that you would like for them to stop?"

The show was going well and I was getting a lot of good, hard political comments.

Finally, a man with a very serious voice came on the line and I repeated the topic to him: "What's the government doing for you that you would like for them to stop?"

In a business-like tone of voice, my caller said, "We must take immediate steps to see that our government stops giving our boys in the Navy saltpeter."

I was completely taken in. I said, "Tell me, sir, why do you regard that as a problem?"

He replied, "Because the Navy gave me some in 1943 and it's just now starting to work."

Not being sure what he would say next, I discontinued the call. When I answered the next call, a woman was on the line, laughing so hard it was almost impossible to tell what she was saying. I said, "What are you laughing at?"

She giggled and said, "I think I know that guy."

I get to meet all sorts of wonderful people by doing a radio talk show, and that's one of the reasons that I have dubbed my callers the "Whackos." They are special people. Sometimes they're funny on purpose and sometimes quite by accident.

One day my friend Dan Fitzpatrick was co-hosting my show. My topic was one that I thought would be good for a few laughs. It was "What is a nerd? What kind of clothes does a nerd wear? Where does a nerd go to college? What is the most common name for a nerd? What type of car does a nerd drive? What is his favorite movie? What kind of job does a nerd have?"

It was a fun show, and most of the callers were in the spirit of the whole thing.

We were getting funny, outrageous answers. About halfway through the show, a young man who said he was twelve years old called.

"Mr. Porch," he said, "I know what a nerd is."

"Good, lay it on me," I replied.

The young caller was very serious, and it was apparent to everyone listening that he was reading the definition for a nerd out of his dictionary.

He started to read, in a flat voice, "Nerd, a noun,

slang for gauche, tacky, a creep, a drip or uncool person. Organ unknown."

When he said, "Organ unknown," Dan and I absolutely collapsed into gales of laughter.

I don't know who the young caller was, but I owe him one thing. Anytime I run into someone that I'm sure is a nerd, I have one thought and one thought only: "Organ unknown!"

In that short three-minute conversation, that wonderful twelve-year-old boy gave me a way to handle some of life's terrible moments.

Recently I was doing battle with a government clerk who could not have found his own fanny with a ten-man working party. As I turned and walked away from his desk, victory was mine. I said, under my breath, "Organ unknown."

Bloody Mary is one of my favorite "Whackos." She has been a regular radio caller for over ten years. We call her Bloody Mary because by her own definition she is our resident drunk.

Truth be known, she drinks a lot less than she lets on. She is a funny, funny lady with a mind so quick that you know she is just waiting for a straight line so she can fire off one of her great lines. She called me one Thanksgiving day several years ago.

I said, "Mary, you sound to me like you may have been drinking."

She shot back, "That don't exactly make you Sherlock Holmes, Luddy. You know full well that I've always 'been drinking.'"

I said, "What's on your mind this beautiful Thanksgiving day, Mary?"

Pardon Me While I Turn Weird

"Well," she said, "I've got a problem that I need some help with."

"Tell us your problem and either me or one of our listeners will see if we can help you."

"Well," she started, "I'm cooking our Thanskgiving dinner, and I made a little mistake. You see, I basted the turkey with vodka rather than the drippings that I was supposed to use."

Trying to be funny, I said, "Okay, Mary, so what's the problem?"

Mary took a deep breath and replied, "Well, the problem is that the damn turkey keeps opening the oven door and turning the heat down."

There has never been a Thanksgiving since that I haven't had a mental picture of that poor drunk turkey turning the heat down on Bloody Mary's oven.

One day my on-the-air topic was superstition. I had opened up the show by saying that I felt everybody was superstitious about something.

It was a very popular topic. We received calls from people about the number thirteen, about walking under ladders, and almost every other superstition under the sun.

In an effort to broaden the topic, I asked one caller, "How do you feel about black cats?" The caller agreed that black cats crossing your path were a sure sign of bad luck.

We had about ten callers, all agreeing that a black cat crossing your path was bad luck.

Finally, my friend M. T. Head called. M. T. always starts his on-the-air calls to me by saying, "This is M. T. Head, Georgia's only auto mechanic and brain surgeon

and the only graduate of Shorty's Agricultural, Mechanical and Medical School, Pit Barbecue Café and Truck Stop, Letohatchie, Alabama 36047."

I said, "M. T., what do you know about superstition?"

He said, "I know one thing. A black cat is not unlucky just walking across your path. But if that same black cat stops in front of you, pulls a gun and says, 'Gimme all your money, Sucker!' then that is definitely bad luck."

I never even knew my next weirdo's name, but I do know that for about six months he was the talk of the United States Marine Corps Air Station, Cherry Point, North Carolina.

He was apparently unhappy with his years in the Marines.

When he was discharged, he caught a taxi to the main gate. He took his seabag outside the gate and emptied all his uniforms into a pile right in front of the guard shack.

With the startled M.P.'s looking on, he poured lighter fluid all over his pile of belongings and set them on fire. Then he started to jump up and down on the flaming clothes, the whole time singing "The Marine Hymn" to the tune of "My Darlin' Clementine."

In his effort to show contempt for the military in general and the Marine Corp in particular, however, he had apparently forgotten that when you are discharged the military gives you travel time to reach home. He was therefore technically still in the service at the time of his seabag cremation.

The M.P.'s walked outside the gate, placed him under arrest, and threw him in the brig. He was court-martialed and was six months late getting home.

I pulled into the service station in a small middle-Georgia town. The operator came walking out of the past towards me. I say walking out of the past because while the rest of the world had moved on into the eighties, it was obvious to me that this attendant would have been right at home in any of the four preceding decades.

He was wearing bib overalls, a plaid long-sleeved shirt and a hat that said "John Deere" on it.

He had a rag in his hands and was wiping them vigorously. He walked up to the driver's side and said what I knew he was going to say: "Can I hep ya?"

"Fill it up, please." He moved to the back of the car and in about thirty seconds reappeared at my window and said, "Check your oil?"

I replied by pulling the hood release.

I was driving a brand-new Ford Thunderbird, and it was fun to watch him as he pulled the three-foot-long dipstick out of the engine. It was obvious by the expression on his face that here was a man impressed by long dipsticks.

He wiped it on the same rag that he had been wiping his hands on, then stuck it back into the engine.

He then reappeared at the window to show me the dipstick. He had a very solemn expression on his face, like a doctor about to tell you that your favorite uncle just died.

Holding the dip stick so that I had to see it, he said, "This dipstick ain't even touchin' your oil."

I decided to have a little fun with him. "Oh, really?" I said. "How much would you charge me for a longer dipstick?"

I thought that he would get a big laugh out of that, but to my surprise he didn't even smile. He just stood there weighing my words, trying to fathom the logic of my question.

He finally spoke. "Why, I don't reckon that would help none," he said. "What you really need is some oil. Besides, I 'spect you got about the longest dipstick they is."

I have often wondered how many times he has told that story to his buddies.

There is a small town in west Georgia located on Highway 78. The natives like to say that it is so small that they don't have a town square . . . they have a town triangle. They have a three-man police force, and the town's most prized possession is its statue in the middle of the main street. The statue is of a Confederate soldier.

One of the three police officers is a slack-jawed old boy named Luther Eugene.

One day Luther Eugene was directing traffic in front of the Confederate statue. When a car with a Vermont license plate and two elderly couples stopped beside him, the driver said, "Pardon me, officer, but could you tell us whose statue that is?"

Luther Eugene was a mouth breather and was obviously a little taken aback by the question. He looked up at the statue for a few seconds, then turned back to the driver of the car and said, "It's ours."

I was sitting at my desk at the radio station when I got a phone call from a P.R.-type.

He told me that a new play was opening in town and

the director was available for an interview (I learned years ago that directors are always available for interviews).

He said the play was *Boys in the Band*. It was a big hit in New York and was opening in Atlanta in the next few days.

I agreed to the interview and thought no more about it.

I knew that *Boys in the Band* had a homosexual theme, but it didn't occur to me that the director would be gay. Not that it bothered me. I had been on the air with many gays before, talking about everything from gay rights to floral arrangements.

I don't think, however, I was ready for this much femininity in any one human being, male or female.

I'm not exaggerating one bit when I tell you that this old boy had more swish than Liz Taylor on the best day of her life. You could tell by his walk, talk and general demeanor that he didn't want anybody to miss the fact that he was gay. You could hear the swish from a hundred yards away. In short, he was the stereotype of every gay joke you ever heard.

The interview was going well in spite of his contrived lisp.

I was avoiding any questions about homosexuality or the gay lifestyle, but it soon became apparent that my guest was not there to talk about his play. He was there to talk about the wonderfulness of his sexual preference and how gays are mistreated in our society.

It took the radio audience a few minutes to catch on to what he was doing, but when they did, they started to call in droves.

He insulted a few of them, and a few of them insulted

him. About thirty minutes into the show, I felt it was a draw, insult wise.

A lady called and started the conversation by identifying herself as a "born-again, Bible-believing Christian." She said that she did not believe in judging people, but that my guest was a piece of slime that was going to bust hell wide open when he died.

Then she said that I was no better than he was because I allowed him on the air. She said that in all likelihood, everyone at the radio station was going to be there too, because we were all guilty of promoting queers.

She was screaming, and you could hear the hate in every syllable.

Finally, I said, "Can I ask you a question?"

She said, "Yes."

"You started our conversation by saying you were a Christian, but it sounds to me like you hate this man. Is that true?"

She said, "I don't hate anyone. I'm a Christian and Christians don't hate. But I'll tell you one thing. If I was your guest, I'd be down on my knees praying for forgiveness."

The guest interrupted her at that point and said, "Sweetie Pie, when I get down on my knees, I've got better things to do than pray."

The caller got real quiet. I can't be sure, but I'd bet a new saddle that she fainted.

My guest told me "ta-ta" and left the radio station singing "I'm in the Mood for Love."

I bet that's why they say, "There's no business like show business."

James was about three years older than the rest of

our teen-aged crowd, and he had dropped out of school after the seventh grade. It was just as well. James was a right nice old boy, but somewhere in James's head two wires didn't touch, and it soon became apparent that school was not his strong suit.

He would do strange things. I remember one time he showed up for school two hours late. When he got there, we were having recess and were playing softball. James stayed until recess was over, then went back home.

In those days, there was no way to treat kids like James, so everyone just sort of agreed that he was different — nothing was going to change that, and there was no need to be too upset.

James didn't have a lazy bone in his body, and while he bounced from job to job, he was always working.

He got himself a job at the neighborhood grocery store. He was about seventeen and the rest of us were thirteen or fourteen.

The owner of the store would leave every day to make home deliveries at three o'clock in the afternoon and would leave James in charge of the store. This was our cue to put our larcenous little brains in gear and see if we could get something free out of good old James.

The scam worked like this. You would go into the store and take a piece of candy to James at the cash register. James would say, "That'll be five cents, please."

Then you would say, "I think I'll swap this candy bar for a big orange drink." You would then stand around the soft-drink box "swiggin" on the Big Orange until it was all gone. Your next move was to start for the front door and in a loud, friendly voice say, "Take it easy, James. I'll see you later."

Ludlow Porch

James would say, "Hold on there a minute. You forgot to pay for your Big Orange drink."

Still walking toward the door, you would say, "Don't you remember, James? I swapped you the candy bar for the drink."

"Yeah," said James, "but you didn't pay for the candy bar."

Going out the door now, you would say, "Yeah, but don't you remember? I didn't eat it."

James would say, "Oh, yeah, for a minute I forgot."

The last time I saw old James, he was working at a gas station. I never think about him that I don't get a little pang of conscience. He was a very nice person. A lot nicer than the rest of us.

I have a lawyer friend who is in his fifties. He is a very handsome man, knows how to dress, and while I think he's pretty much harmless, he does have an eye for the ladies. He is what you would consider one of your garden variety, silver-tongued devils.

One day we were on an elevator together when the door opened and a very beautiful young lady of about twenty-five summers got on. I knew my friend was attracted to her because he immediately sucked in his stomach.

The elevator door closed and my friend said, "Hello, Beautiful. Where have you been all of my life?"

The young lady never paused and in a very sweet voice said, "Well, for the first half of it I wasn't born."

The only sound you could hear after that was my laughter. She got off in the lobby and walked out of our lives forever, but I don't think either one of us will ever forget her.

When Insurance Can't Protect You

A GOOD PART OF my adult life was spent as an insurance adjuster. It was a very valuable time for me because I think it gave me the best possible insight into human behavior. I am convinced that insurance adjusters see the world at its best and at its worst.

I also became convinced that many Americans consider insurance companies "fair game." People who would never, under any circumstances, steal a dime from their fellow man have no trouble at all socking it to an insurance company.

I received a call one day from an insurance agent who reported that one of his insureds had suffered some fire damage.

My heart skipped a beat when he told me the name of his client. It was a local deli, owned and operated by three brothers.

The word around the office was that these brothers actually ran a deli as a hobby and made insurance claims for a living. That was, of course, an exaggeration, but only a slight one.

I immediately got one of the brothers on the telephone. When he realized he had the adjuster on the phone, he started to cough. His performance would have put Bette Davis to shame.

He said, "Oh, thank God, you've called. The fire was awful. The smoke is unbearable. It's a wonder we're not all dead. When can you come and check out the damage (cough, cough, cough)? I think I've got smoke in my lungs. The whole place is a shambles."

I said, "I'll be right there." I jumped in my car and lit out.

I was fully expecting to find the fire department still there and the roof of the delicatessen collapsed. You can imagine my confusion, then, when I arrived and found the place open and doing business as usual. I got there around lunch time, and the place was crowded with customers.

It was an old building, and the place had not been painted since Admiral Halsey was a boot.

I finally made my way through the lunch-time crowd and found one of the owners in the kitchen. When I told him who I was, he started to cough and tell me about the blazing inferno his deli had been only minutes before. I said, "Exactly where was the fire?"

He answered, "My God, it was awful (cough, cough). It's a miracle we weren't all burned alive."

I said, "Where was the fire?"

He said, "Words cannot explain (cough, cough) what it's like to live through something like that. My whole life (cough, cough) passed in front of my eyes."

I said, "I understand, but *where* was the fire?"

"It was there," he finally said, "in the stove." He pointed to an old grease-laden forty-year-old, four-burner gas stove.

"It doesn't look damaged," I said. "It just looks old."

He said, "Of course, it doesn't look damaged. The fire was on the inside in the oven."

I walked over, opened the oven door and looked inside. It was black and dirty, but otherwise looked okay.

I said, "Did the fire department make a report?"

"Fire department?" he screamed. "What fire department? There wasn't time to call the fire department. We had to put it out. We could have been roasted alive waiting for the lousy fire department."

I said, "Okay, what are your damages?"

He said, "Well, first off, we must have a new stove. That one was like brand-new. Second, the whole place has got to be painted. Kitchen, dining area, the works. And, third, you owe me $540.00 for the meat that was in the oven when it caught on fire."

I said, "Can I see the meat?"

"We put it in the alley behind the deli."

I said, "Okay, can I just go out and count it for the insurance records?"

He said, "No, you can't do that."

"Why not?" I asked.

"'Cause an old bum came along and took it all away (cough, cough)."

I finally settled by buying them a new stove, having the walls cleaned (not painted) and giving them $200.00 for some nonexistent meat. He was happy, and I felt like I had a little better insight into why insurance premiums were going up.

Mr. O'Brien was a retired telephone-company employee. He was a delightful old gentleman, very polite and very soft spoken.

He was a close friend of his agent, and I had met him at lunch one day. During lunch his agent had told him, "If you should ever, God forbid, have a automobile accident, you should call Ludlow and report it to him at once because his company is your liability carrier."

I thought nothing more about it until my phone rang about six months later.

The conversation went like this:

"Hello, Lud?"

"Yes, sir."

"This is Mr. O'Brien."

"How are you?"

"I'm fine."

"You know, Lud, my agent told me to call you if I ever had an accident, so I thought I'd better give you a buzz."

"What kind of an accident have you had, Mr. O'Brien? Nothing serious, I hope."

"Oh, heavens no. I was just parking my car downtown and backed into this parked car."

"Much damage?"

"Oh, no. Just some damage to his bumper."

"That's good, Mr. O'Brien. This doesn't sound like a big deal. Why don't you and the other man exchange I.D.'s and I'll call him later and arrange to get his car fixed."

"Thanks a lot, Ludlow."

"My pleasure, Mr. O'Brien."

"I don't think it will cost too much to get the parking meter fixed."

"What parking meter, Mr. O'Brien?"

"The one his car hit when I backed into him."

"Much damage?"

"Oh, no, just minor."

"Okay, Mr. O'Brien. I'll contact the city and arrange to pay to repair the parking meter."

"Thanks very much, Ludlow."

"You're very welcome, Mr. O'Brien. You take care now, and I'll see you soon."

"I don't think the man was seriously injured."

"What man, Mr. O'Brien?"

"The one that the top of the parking meter flew off and hit."

"Do you know his name, Mr. O'Brien?"

"No, I didn't have time to get it, but I'm sure the ambulance attendant will know his name."

"The ambulance attendant?"

"Yes, they took him away in the ambulance."

"Where are you, Mr. O'Brien?"

He told me that he was in a phone booth just a few feet from where the accident happened.

When I got there, I found out that he had been backing his car into a horizontal parking place, the gas pedal had stuck, and he had plowed into the car behind him, knocking it onto the curb and into a parking meter. The top of the parking meter was knocked from the post, flew through the air and hit a man who was walking down the street in the stomach. A policeman witnessed the accident and said the pedestrian caught the parking meter in his gut like a basketball. The injury was minor, but I will never forget Mr. O'Brien's explanation of it.

Some of the most interesting hours I ever spent were those negotiating with plaintiffs' attorneys.

I soon learned that most lawyers are lazy when it

comes to investigating an accident. The average plaintiff's lawyer simply orders a police report, sends his client to a doctor and then waits for settlement time.

On the other hand, insurance adjusters are required by the companies they represent to make full and complete investigations. In addition to police reports, adjusters take statements from all involved parties, photograph and sometimes diagram accident scenes, and get complete medical reports on injuries.

I was negotiating a case with a hotshot plaintiff's attorney in Birmingham, Alabama. It was a case with a minor injury to his client and a case with absolutely no legal liability.

He knew that it was a case with little settlement value and that legally he didn't have a leg to stand on. He also knew that I would pay something just to keep from spending the money that a defense of this case would cost.

He decided to be charming. I was ushered into his office, given coffee and the royal treatment. He talked about everything under the sun except what I was there to talk about.

I was just waiting for him to go into his Clarence Darrow routine. Finally he stopped smiling and said, "Okay, let's talk some business." Then he went into his act.

He sat back, took a big drag on his cigar and said, "Ludlow . . . you don't mind if I call you Ludlow, do you? This is a very serious case, and if this case ever goes to jury, they're going to hand down a sizeable plaintiff's verdict.

"However, my client needs some money, so I've decided to give you a break. But before I give you a demand, there is something you should know about me. I don't horsetrade and I don't haggle. Now, I want $1,500 to settle this case. That is my bottom dollar. That is absolutely the least I will consider. I won't consider a penny less. As a matter of fact, $1,500 is the only amount I'd be willing to submit to my client. That's it. $1,500. Take it or leave it. What's your decision?"

I said, "I'll give you $250."

He said, "Could you make it $300?"

We settled for $300.00.

There is one lawyer in Atlanta who has never, to my knowledge, filed a lawsuit.

The story goes in insurance circles that as a very young lawyer he sued someone and lost and had never filed another suit. I don't know if that's true or not, but I have always believed it.

His attack is to get all of his medical information together and come to the office of the adjuster and not leave until you settle the case. He will literally spend the day with an adjuster until it's a matter of settling with him or killing him.

I have always felt that he performs a valuable service for his clients. Admittedly, he doesn't get as much money for his clients as some of his silk-suit colleagues, but neither does he drag a case out, trying to build its values for two or three years.

Insurance companies are strange creatures. At one time or another, I represented thirty-six different insurance companies.

The adjuster reports directly to a claims examiner. For the most part the examiners to whom I reported were my friends, and we had a free and easy relationship.

I think the ones that I enjoyed the most, however, were those who had no sense of humor and took the business of insurance far too seriously.

I have always believed that anything you do for a living should be fun, and I made sure to keep that attitude alive and well, even when the people who were paying me doubted my sanity.

One company that I represented had a report that they expected you to file within twenty-four hours of the accident.

I had no problem with that, but there was no room on their form for a complete statement of the facts. I soon managed to make this form into a game between me and my humorless examiner.

I had to report on a tragic accident that occurred when an employee was killed by a freight elevator.

I looked at the tiny space marked "Description of Accident" and had my secretary type in this description: "Claimant looked up elevator shaft to see if elevator was coming. It was."

The examiner did not see the humor in my description.

On another occasion, I wrote, "Vehicle damage to insured's kitchen."

I got a telex the next day from the apparently irritated examiner. It said, "Please advise how vehicle got into insured's kitchen."

I sent my reply immediately. It said, "He went to the dining room and turned left."

In one of my reports to my humorless friend, I had neglected to tell him the age of a claimant with a broken leg.

His memo said, "How old claimant?"

I wrote back, "Old claimant not feeling well, leg broken."

One of the more interesting characters I met while in the insurance business worked right in my office.

She was a great secretary and also one of the most gullible people I ever knew. Her gullibility made her the perfect foil for every office prank.

One day I bought a cigar in a glass case. I smoked the cigar after lunch, on my way down the hall leading to my office. I stopped by the water fountain and filled the glass container with water. I replaced the plastic cap and dried it off with my handkerchief. When I walked into my office, I said, "I bought a present for your kids. It's the latest fad. I hope they enjoy it."

I handed her the cigar tube and, with a straight face, walked into my office.

I knew she couldn't stand the suspense for long, and in about ten minutes she walked into my office and said, "I don't want you to think I'm not grateful, but would you mind telling me what this is?"

I said, "It's the newest fad from the pet world. It's invisible guppies."

She paused and then said, "Well, that's very nice, but what do you feed them?"

"Fish food," I answered with a straight face.

"How do you know if they are eating?"

"When the food is gone," I said.

She thanked me again.

The next morning she arrived at work all smiles. She came into my office and said, "I have a confession to make. Yesterday I thought you were kidding about the invisible guppies, so when I got home I called three different pet stores. The first two said they had never heard of invisible guppies, but the third one said that they had become his biggest seller. He said that they were in such demand that he was sold out. I asked him how his children enjoyed them. He said they like them a lot but he felt they were a little young to enjoy them to the fullest."

Over the next couple of weeks, she apparently told all of her friends about the invisible guppies.

I'm not sure who finally convinced her that her leg was being pulled, but one morning she brought me the water-filled cigar tube, handed it to me and said, "You're an awful man. I feel like a complete fool. Everyone I know thinks I'm crazy."

I held the cigar tube up to the light and said, "My God, they're all dead. What did you do to them?"

She stomped out of my office mumbling something about my ancestors.

She was not only the world's best secretary, she was also an actress of some renown. Whenever she needed the afternoon off, she would always give me a sure-fire reason like, "I'm having brain surgery at three o'clock. Okay if I get off about two o'clock?" If we weren't busy, I would always let her off.

However, on the days that I could not let her off, she would give a performance that was worthy of an Oscar.

One morning she asked if she could have the afternoon off. I explained to her that it was a bad time since we were absolutely covered up with work.

She didn't say anymore about it but was awfully quiet for the balance of the morning.

A friend of mine came by and we went out to lunch.

When Insurance Can't Protect You

When we got back, my secretary was laid out in the middle of the office floor, doing her best to appear semi-conscious. There was a file drawer pulled out and files were laying all on top of her.

It scared my friend, but I recognized it immediately as one of her performances and a way to get the afternoon off.

I kneeled down beside her and said, "Are you all right?"

In a sleepy, far-off voice, she said, "My back, it's my back."

I said, "Do you want me to send for an ambulance?"

She said, "No, I'll be all right. I think."

I said, "Do you want me to help you up, or would you like for me to put your typewriter down here?"

"You're just impossible!" she said in a loud voice. "Can't you see that I could be paralyzed from the waist down?"

I said, "No, I can't see that, but if you think I'm buying this phony accident, you must think I'm paralyzed from the neck up."

She got right up and went to work, all the time mumbling something about joining a union.

You meet strange, weird people wherever you go in the insurance business.

I worked with a safety engineer in Birmingham named Murphy. I have often felt that engineers, like professional photographers, live in a world all their own. I'm not saying that they're bad people, but I do believe that they don't plant their corn in straight rows.

Murph was about sixty years old and had never married. He was your typical, set-in-his-ways bachelor.

The office manager was named Stanley, and Murph hated him worse than a farmer hates a fox. He would go to any lengths to pick a fight with poor Stanley.

One morning Murphy was sitting at his desk working when Stanley came in. He passed Murphy's desk and said, "Good morning, Murph."

Murphy got up from his desk and came stomping into my office. "Did you hear what Stanley just said to me?"

I said, "Yeah, I heard."

Murph said, "What do you think he meant by that?"

"I'm not sure, but I think he meant 'Good Morning.'"

"Oh, no!" Murph shot back. "He's got something on his mind. I think I'm going to go into his office right now and ask him what the hell he meant, and if he doesn't tell me I'm going to punch him in his ugly mouth."

I said, "Let me see if I've got this straight, Murph. You're about to go into Stanley's office and punch him in the mouth for telling you 'Good Morning'?"

"It wasn't so much what he said, it was the way he said it," Murph said.

"Murph, do you know how crazy that sounds?"

He leaned across my desk and through clinched teeth said, "I should have known better than to talk to you about anything. You don't have any emotions. You're always so damned logical."

I said, "Look, Murph, don't get me in the middle. You go in there and beat Stanley up, and when the police come to get you, I'll go to court to testify that he did indeed say 'Good Morning' to you."

Murph stomped out of my office saying, "You management types always stick together."

When Insurance Can't Protect You

Murphy's exploits were many and varied. I soon learned that if you dealt much with old Murph, his combative attitude would just about drive you crackers.

One morning about 3:30 A.M. my phone rang. Whenever my phone rings at 3:30 A.M., I always assume that someone is dead. I frankly don't remember ever getting any good news at that time of the day.

I made my way to the phone and answered with a sleepy, half panicked "Hello."

It was Murph. In a cheery, drunk voice, he said, "Did I wake you?"

I said, "Of course, you woke me. It's 3:30 in the morning."

Murph shot back, "Well, if you're going to be snotty about it just forget I called," and with that he slammed the phone down.

I went back to bed. My wife said, "Who was that?"

I said, "It was Murphy."

"What did he want?"

"I don't know. I'll find out tomorrow."

We went back to sleep. At 3:45 the phone rang again.

"Hello, Lud, this is Murph. Look, Lud, I'm really sorry that I hung up on you."

"That's okay, Murph. What do you want?"

"Before I tell you what I want, you've got to tell me that you accept my apology."

"I accept your apology. Now what do you want?"

"I need for you to come get me out of jail. Will you do it?"

"Certainly I'll do it. But why are you in jail?"

He shouted into the phone, "What gives you the right

to stick your ugly nose into my private affairs? You can go straight to hell!" And he hung up on me again.

The next morning I went to work. I decided on the way that if Murph gave me any trouble about our phone conversation, I was going to find a way to put a bomb in his shorts.

He was already there when I arrived. He followed me into my office, closed the door behind him and said, "Can I ask you a question?"

"Shoot," I said, immediately regretting my choice of words.

He said, "Did I call you last night?"

"You don't remember?"

"Well," he said, "to tell you the truth, I had a little too much to drink, and I seem to remember having a phone conversation with you."

"No, it wasn't me, Murph. It wasn't me."

He said, "You're not gonna believe this, but the police put me in jail for D.U.I. and I called Stanley and he got me out."

I said, "Boy, that was nice of him."

"Hell, the bastard let me cool my heels in jail for almost an hour before he got me out." Then he took a deep breath and said, "I'll never understand why Stanley hates me so."

A claims adjuster gets a liberal education when working with contractors. There's no way to avoid contact with them when you make your living as an adjuster.

These are the folks who do the repair work for the fire damage, water damage or other hazards that your company has insured against.

I should point out that in every city there are several honest, dependable, above-board, hard-working contractors. I should also point out that for every one of these honest, dependable, above-board, hard-working contractors, there are three sleaze-ball, crooked, underhanded vampires.

Handling a claim with a contractor should be a simple process. All the adjuster is trying to do is to establish the damage and have it repaired at a reasonable price. I said reasonable, not necessarily cheap.

Most adjusters will tell you that the crooked contractors I'm talking about try every trick in the book to get filthy rich on every job they undertake. While they're seeking their fortune, they do everything humanly possible to make the homeowner's life a living hell.

If they can't pull the wool over the adjuster's eyes by lying about prices or the number of square feet in a room, then they will try to bribe him.

Most adjusters have been offered everything from whiskey to women to cash on the barrelhead.

While the following is not an insurance story, I think it will make my point and also highlight one of life's little victories.

There was a crooked contractor a few years back. His favorite way to get business was to give parties in his office, serve whiskey and show thirty-year-old skin flicks and invite adjusters to come by for all this so-called fun.

Over the time I knew of him, he must have operated under about ten different names.

My great Aunt Jill owned rental property all over town. She was very rich, very tight, and could be mean as a snake with an abscessed fang when she thought she was being cheated.

She contracted with this sleaze-bag to put a new roof on a rental house she owned, and some way or another she was convinced that he had cheated her out of six-hundred dollars.

She had tried repeatedly to recoupe her six-hundred but of course had no luck.

She investigated him completely and found out where his office was. She also found out that he had spent thousands and thousands of dollars putting a cabinet shop in the basement of the office building he rented.

She called me and asked if I would intervene on her behalf and try to talk him into giving her the money that she was convinced he had stolen from her.

I decided to try and reason with him since I really didn't know the whole story, but I did know I was dealing with a thief and a crazy old lady who would do almost anything for six hundred dollars.

I explained to him that I wasn't sticking my nose where it didn't belong, but she was convinced that he owed her money.

He said, "I don't owe her a dime."

"Look," I countered, "I don't know if you do or not. The point is, she thinks you do and to her that's the same thing."

He said again, "I don't owe her a dime and that's that."

"Look, she *is* rich and she *is* mean when provoked, and she's about half nuts. Now, I'm convinced that if you gave her six hundred dollars it would be money well spent. Take my word for it, you don't want my Aunt Jill as an enemy."

He said, "I told you once, not a dime. And you can tell that crazy old bat I said so, and if that doesn't suit her, I'll see her in court."

"You don't really mean that," I said.

"Yes, I do. You give her my message."

"Okey dokey," I said, "but don't say I didn't warn you."

I told Aunt Jill exactly what he said. She took it very calmly. She just smiled and said, "Thanks for trying. I'll handle it from here on out."

Handle it she did. The first thing she did was to buy the building where his office and cabinet shop were located. In accordance with the terms of the lease, she gave him thirty days to be out. He called her and said there was no way he could move all the cabinet-making equipment out in thirty days. She said there was no rush, but for any time after thirty days his equipment was in *her* cabinet shop, the rent would be six-hundred dollars a day. I'm not sure how this story ended, but I am sure that Aunt Jill won the battle and the war.

When you spend as many years doing anything as I did in the insurance business, you have many peaks and valleys. You work with and grow to know all types. Some you love and some you would just as soon forget.

If I had to pick out the top three characters, I mean real characters, that I ever met in my life, Mr. James L. Rankin of Decatur, Alabama, would certainly be among them.

Jim has been a highly successful insurance agent for many, many years.

When I first met him, I was about twenty-five years old and he was approaching sixty. I was warned by people I worked with that he was eccentric and could be difficult. I had just been promoted to claims manager of our Birmingham office, and I knew it was important that I have good relations with my company's independent insurance agents.

I had no need to worry. Jim and I started a friendship on our first meeting that has lasted until this day. He was and is a character. As they say, it takes one to know one.

Jim left the University of Tennessee in the late 1930's and moved to the beautiful Tennessee valley town of Decatur. But moving to Alabama didn't change his football loyalties. He is probably the No. 1 Tennessee football fan in the country.

He will readily admit that during football season his insurance agency has to run itself because he thinks only of how the Big Orange will fare from week to week.

Jim had an accountant who was also a big Tennessee football fan. Since they both lived in Alabama football country, they not only shared a love for everything Tennessee but also a deep hatred for Alabama football.

One beautiful fall day Mr. Rankin took his elderly accountant to Birmingham to watch their Big Orange play the hated Crimson Tide. Legion Field was packed as it always is when the Tide is playing. Fortunately, their tickets were right in the middle of the Tennessee fans.

It was a tremendous game with the lead changing hands several times.

Midway through the third quarter, a Tennessee player stopped a Tide back trying to sweep the end. It was a bone-crushing tackle that you could hear all over Birmingham. The accountant turned to Mr. Rankin and said, "Jim, I've been following Tennessee football for almost fifty years, and that without a doubt is the finest tackle I've ever seen."

A middle-aged lady sitting on the row in front of them, wearing a mink stole and a pill-box hat, turned around and said in a soft Southern drawl, "That was my son who made that tackle."

The accountant said, "Well, I'll tell you one thing, lady, that son of a bitch can flat play football!"

Mr. Rankin was a great animal lover. He owned a boxer dog named Coke, who was his pride and joy.

The dog weighed well over one-hundred pounds and, like most boxers, never quite got over being a puppy. He was so rambunctious that the only way you could walk him was with a choker collar, because no matter how fast you walked, old Coke wanted to go faster.

It was a nightly ritual for Mr. Rankin to walk Coke after supper, rain or shine. Mr. Rankin lived out of town a ways and there were no street lights.

One particularly dark night they were out for a walk, and as usual old Coke was straining and pulling against the choker chain. The faster Mr. Rankin walked, the harder Coke pulled.

Finally, Mr. Rankin said, "Okay, big boy, if you want to run we'll just do it." He broke into a slow jog.

Coke loved it, but he continued to pull on the leash. So Mr. Rankin started to jog faster. It was the first time in forty years that he had done any running, and he had almost forgotten the fun of it.

He was caught up in it as they approached home, and Mr. Rankin decided to put on a final burst of speed. He was wide-open now, his long legs taking giant strides. There they were running flat out, Coke in the lead, Mr. Rankin holding the leash and running like an Olympian sprinter through the pitch-black Alabama night.

Suddenly Mr. Rankin felt Coke leave the ground. He knew the dog had jumped something but it was too dark to tell just what. He realized that whatever it was, he was too close and running too fast to stop. He reasoned that as foolish as it seemed his only choice was to jump too.

With all his might, he leaped as high and as far as he could.

When he landed, he hit right in the middle of the wheelbarrow that his gardener had left in the yard. He fell, according to his own calculation, for about forty-five minutes.

He was not seriously hurt, but he was skinned and bruised. When he made it into the house, Mrs. Rankin said, "What happened to you?"

"I don't want to talk about it," he said.

"Where is Coke?"

Mr. Rankin said, "I don't know. Last time I saw him he was headed for Cullman at about seventy-five miles per hour."

When the Chrysler Corporation came out with their new Imperial in the early sixties, it was considered the fanciest luxury car on the road. In spite of its then-high price tag of about five thousand dollars, Mr. Rankin had to have one. It was a beauty. It was a four-door and as long as a freight train.

When it was brand-new, he had to drive from Decatur to Birmingham on business. He stopped in the small Alabama town of Hartselle to get gas.

The attendant at the small gas station was a black youngster, about fourteen years old. While the pump was running, he busied himself washing the windshield.

It was apparently the fanciest car he had ever seen, and he was full of questions about it.

"What kind of car is this?" he asked.

"It's called an Imperial," Mr. Rankin answered.

"Show do be a pretty car," he mused. "How fast do you reckon this car will go?"

"I don't have any idea," Mr. Rankin replied.

His curiosity was unlimited. "How much a car like this cost?"

"Oh, about five thousand dollars," Mr. Rankin said.

The young man stopped wiping the windshield and in open-mouthed disbelief said, "Schhhhh, you can buy a Cadillac for dat."

Many of the people an insurance adjuster meets are a little embarrassed because their claim resulted from something dumb they did.

Like the maid in a beautiful Atlanta home who plugged the vacuum cleaner into a 220-volt air-conditioning outlet. It, of course, burned up the cleaner.

When I asked her to tell me what happened, her reply was simple and to the point. She said, "When the juice hit it, it came alive."

When a hospital has a report for their insurance company, it's called an incident report rather than an accident report. I'm not sure why, but I always suspected it was part of most hospitals' effort to convince the world that they don't make mistakes and therefore are above accidents.

One incident report read under "Describe incident": "R.N. gave patient a Fleets enema by mouth."

If you have ever had a Fleets enema, you can just imagine what the poor patient went through.

The next line on the incident report asked the question, "How did patient react to incident?"

The answer given was, "Patient started to vomit almost immediately." Whoever wrote that was sure a master of understatement.

I'll never forget the hospital incident report that came across my desk complete with a long signed statement from the involved employee, an orderly.

The orderly had apparently gotten his charts mixed up and gone into a room where a man was getting ready to be discharged. The man was very happy to be getting out of the hospital. He was sick and tired of being stuck and pushed and pulled by what he regarded as a bunch of strangers.

When the orderly entered the room with an enema bottle, the man dressing to go home asked, "What do you want?"

The orderly said, "I'm here to give you this enema."

"There must be some mistake," said the patient. "I'm being discharged in a few minutes."

The orderly was sure he was right. He said, "You ain't going no where until you've had this enema."

His last remark pushed the poor man over the edge of reason. He looked the orderly right in the eye and said, "If you look at me closely, you will see that we are about the same size."

The orderly said, "What does that have to do with anything?"

"The only point I'm trying to make," the patient said,

"is that if we get into a fight here, you are just about as apt as I am to get that enema."

The last comment convinced the orderly that it would probably be a good idea to recheck the chart.

The patient made a big fuss about it and thus the incident report.

When it comes to married couples fighting, the truth is much, much stranger than fiction.

A case was reported to my office for investigation once where a lady had followed her womanizing husband. She followed him straight to his girlfriend's house and then followed them to a beer joint. She waited outside for several hours while they danced and had a good deal to drink.

Next she followed them to a dark and lonely lovers' lane-type dirt road where she observed from a distance as they got into the back seat together. She waited for a few minutes, getting madder and madder as the seconds ticked by.

When she could stand it no longer, she cranked up her car and drove into the back of her philandering husband's parked vehicle.

The result was two badly damaged cars and a young lady who sustained a rather severe bite at the exact moment of impact.

The wife was very candid and freely told me all the facts. She said her only regret was that she had not been driving a tank.

The adjuster's stock in trade is the signed statement. He spends countless hours hearing people's version of an accident and then reducing that version to writing.

Ludlow Porch

You soon learn that what people say and the actual facts are sometimes not related.

For example, when they say, "All I want is what's coming to me," they usually mean a little place in the country and a college education for their children.

When they say, "I only had two beers," they really mean that they were so drunk they were driving from the back seat.

When they say, "Let's be fair," what they mean is, "You be fair and I'll handle the rape."

When they say, "My car was a cream puff," they usually mean it had 400,000 miles on it and most of them were on a taxi line.

When they say, "I stopped at the stop sign and looked both ways before proceeding," they usually mean, "I ran the stop sign."

When they say, "It's the kind of thing that could have happened to anyone," they usually mean that since the beginning of time it's never happened to anyone else.

When they say, "The ring I lost once belonged to a millionaire," they usually mean his name was Mr. Woolworth.

When they say, "That sofa was brand-new. We just got it," they mean we found it last week in a Dempsey dumpster.

When they say it was a valuable antique, it means they found it in a Cracker Jack box.

We hear a lot about how crooked insurance companies are, making a fortune off the poor policyholder, but take it from someone who has been on both sides of the fence: Insurance companies are the victim more often than they are the criminal.

The Old Folks Tell It Straight

I'M CRAZY ABOUT OLD people. Some of the greatest wisdom of the ages has been given to me by old people, and many of my favorite people throughout my life have been on social security or headed that way.

I'm not real sure why that is. It's more than the fact that they're smarter than the rest of us. I think I like their plain-spoken attitude. They have lived long enough to know what life is all about, and they normally don't mince words.

My friend Sarah summed up her approach to old age by saying, "I never wanted to get old, but once I saw that it was inevitable, I decided to just get as damn old as I could."

Plain, to the point, honest and wise.

That, I think, is what draws me most to old people. They have lived long enough to realize they don't have to fake it anymore. They can just be themselves.

One time I was driving in North Alabama. It had been raining for nearly a week, and all the news was about what the rain was doing to the crops and about flooding in the low-lying areas.

I decided that I would stop and get a soft drink.

Between beats of my wipers, I saw an old country store on the side of the road.

I parked as close as I could so I could run in without getting too wet. There was a roof that ran from the front of the store out over the gas pumps. I jumped out of my car and made a dash for that roof. Once under it, I spotted for the first time an old man sitting on a soft-drink flat, leaning back against the front of the wooden store. He was whittling and never even looked up at me.

I said, "Do you think it's ever going to quit raining?"

Without looking up, he said, "Always has."

What a line. He had lived long enough not to be worried about something as silly as rain, and when I asked him what he must have considered to be a dumb question, he gave me an absolutely honest answer.

I guess honesty is something that you develop with the passing years. I earn a large part of my daily bread as an after-dinner speaker.

Once I was asked to speak at a social club in North Carolina. The club was made up of senior citizens who had "made theirs" and retired. The average age was about seventy-five, and these folks were the cream of that town's society. It was a black-tie affair, and the parking lot was crammed full of new Cadillacs.

When it came time for me to be introduced, the M.C. for the evening stood up and approached the rostrum. He was at least ninety years old. He was holding the bio material that my agent had sent him to introduce me with.

He stopped in front of the microphone and tapped on a glass with his spoon. When the audience got quiet, he cleared his throat and said, "It says here that our guest speaker is Ludlow Porch. I've never heard of him, but I guess he'll be all right." Then he sat down.

There was an old gentleman who lived in my hometown named F. A. Perry. Nobody called him F. A. or even Mr. Perry; he was known to everyone as Sgt. Perry. He was beyond the shadow of a doubt the most interesting character I have ever met.

He had joined the army as a very young man and stayed in until his retirement. Once out of the army, he went to work for the Federal Reserve Bank and stayed there for twenty years and retired again. He was still less than sixty-five. When he finally reached sixty-five and became eligible for social security, he enjoyed telling everyone that he was three times retired.

He was fit as a fiddle and showed a love for life that men half his age looked at with envy.

He was still too young at heart to retire completely, so he opened a small store behind his house. It was not a big deal. Milk, bread, soft drinks and snacks for the school kids who passed every day.

The story, as he told it, went like this: One day he got tired of running the little store, so he went in his house, got the dictionary down from the shelf and looked up the word *retire*. The dictionary said it meant to "fall back, cease to labor." Sgt. Perry said he closed the book and said, "By God, I've retired again."

He went to the store, put a padlock on the door and immediately had some business cards printed that said, "SGT. F. A. PERRY, FOUR TIMES RETIRED AND ONCE FIRED."

He had only two secrets from his friends: He would

never tell anyone who fired him and he would never tell his age.

But he loved to tell stories of his army days. His memory was great, and he was a master storyteller.

He was one of the last living men called out against the Indians, and he told that story often.

His favorite story revolved around the death of the company bootlegger when he was stationed at Fort Dodge, Kansas.

In those days there was no stigma attached to being a bootlegger. It was before the days when the federal government was so interested in who made and sold whiskey, and every military base had their own bootlegger either on the military post or just a short walk away.

When the bootlegger died, it was the dead of winter, and because the ground was frozen so hard, it took about three days to get the grave dug.

The bootlegger was a much beloved member of the military community. It was his practice to give credit to anyone who could not come up with the price of a bottle. He had even been known to make loans to the soldiers at Fort Dodge who were "up against it" and needed a few dollars till pay day.

It was therefore a full military funeral when it came time to bury their beloved bootlegger.

They were all standing at attention at the gravesite when the captain said in a loud voice, "Men, we are here today to pay our last farewell to our beloved friend, the bootlegger. There is one here among us who knew him best of all."

Then the captain said in a loud, commanding voice, "Sgt. Murphy, front and center."

A hush fell over the troops because every man there knew that Sgt. Murphy was a grizzled, tough old sargeant without a sentimental bone in his ramrod-straight body. They could not imagine any words of sentiment coming from the mouth of Sgt. Murphy.

Every eye was on him as he crunched his way over the frozen ground. When he reached the head of the grave, he did not pause for even a second. Standing at attention, he barked, "Uncoverrr." Every hat came off at once.

Sgt. Murphy's eyes swept the troops. When he was convinced that they were all uncovered and standing at attention, he continued in the same loud drill-sargeant voice.

"When we come into this world, we are naked and bare. When we die, we go we know not where. But if we've been all right here, we'll be all right there. Throw the dirt in."

I didn't see Sgt. Perry for several years before he died.

Then one day a mutual friend called me and told me that my dear friend had answered his last muster. It made me want to cry, and I didn't know how to respond to the bad news. Finally, I said, "He's been all right here. He'll be all right there."

A Nickel Spent Is A Tearful Event

IT WOULD NOT BE accurate to say that my friend Tom is cheap. It would be more accurate to say that he has spent a lifetime trying to find a way to go through each day without spending a dime.

Let me explain up front that Tom is not poor and has never been poor. He is just cheap and has always been cheap.

Tom and I grew up together. I first realized Tom's affliction during our teen years.

We were both about sixteen. He called me on the phone and said, "My girl's cousin is in town. How would you like a blind date?"

I said, "Not me, Big Daddy. The last blind date I had looked like Yogi Berra. Besides, I'm broke and payday is almost a week away."

He said, "You've got to help me, man. My girl's mother won't let her out of the house unless we take her cousin. Look, if you'll go with us, I'll pay for everything. It won't cost you a dime."

I said, "What does the cousin look like?"

"She's beautiful, man, absolutely beautiful."

Still suspicious, I asked again, "And you do

have some money?"

Sensing a victory, he became more excited. "I'm loaded. I just got paid and I've got a pocket full of money," he went on. "If you'll do this for me," he promised, "I'll never forget it."

I finally said, "Okay, it's against my better judgment, but if it's that important to you, I'll do it. But she better look as good as you say."

I spent the rest of the day dreading the blind date.

That night Tom picked me up and we drove to his girl's home. We were ushered into the parlor and told that the girls would be right in.

I didn't want to be there and toyed with the idea of feigning an epiletic seizure. When I was almost ready to go into my act, the girls walked in.

My blind date was the most beautiful girl I had ever seen. It was lust at first sight.

She was about 5'3" and had beautiful honey-blonde hair fixed in a pony tail. She had that peaches-and-cream complexion that you always hear about. In short, she was what every sixteen-year-old boy dreams about.

We got to the restaurant after what seemed to be the shortest drive in history. I was being so grown up and charming that you wouldn't believe it.

More than anything else on earth, I wanted to impress this ivory-skinned teen goddess that Jesus had sent to me.

I opened the car door for her and tried to do everything that I thought Errol Flynn might do under similar circumstances. We had a nice dinner, and my table manners had never been better.

It didn't bother me at all that I didn't have any money.

After all, my best friend Tom had already said that he would pick up the tab for the evening.

When we finished dessert, the waitress brought the check. Tom picked it up and started to study it.

More anxious than ever to impress my date, I said in a cool, low voice, "I'll take care of that, Tom."

Without a second's hesitation, Tom said, "Okay," and handed me the check.

In the next fifteen seconds, my whole life passed in front of my eyes.

Here I was more in love than Romeo, looking at a sizeable dinner check and not a dime to my name.

I said, "Tom, I seem to have something in my eye. Would you mind stepping in the men's room and helping me get it out?" Then ever chivalrous, I said, "Will you excuse us, ladies?"

Smiling as we left the table, Tom and I went into the men's room.

When the door closed behind us, I turned to Tom and said, "Give me all the money you have on you or I'll kill you."

He said, "What?"

"Look, Buckethead, you just embarrassed me in front of the woman I love. Now, give me all your money so I can pay the check, or I'm going to drown you in a urinal."

Even in the face of such a threat, he hesitated before giving me the money. That was my first real experience with Tom as a tightwad.

If anything, the years have made his money-grubbing even worse.

I can expect to hear from him about once a month. He starts by saying, "Let's go to lunch. I've got this fabulous restaurant that you must try."

I have learned over the years that when he says he has a fabulous restaurant, he really means that he found a coupon for a free meal in a magazine. He would drive miles and miles to cash in on a free coupon.

The reason he called me so often for lunch was that most of the coupons were of the buy-one-get-one-free variety. That meant that I would buy one and he would get one free.

Under this strange arrangement, I have eaten in some of the worst restaurants in the free world.

I'll never forget the time that Tom had a coupon for what he described as a gourmet Mexican restaurant. I knew that I had made a bad dining decision when Tom drove up in front of the place and a large yellow neon sign proclaimed, "El Nas Too Dough Mexican Restaurant." The windows were so dirty that you could barely see inside.

I said, "Tom, unless you're heavily armed, there is no way that you're going to get me inside that place."

He said, "Don't be silly. You'd have to drive all the way to Mexico to find a restaurant like this one."

"That's what I'm afraid of," I said. "I betcha they got roaches in there bigger than cats."

He said, "Hey, you got to go in. Today's Wednesday."

"What's that got to do with anything?"

Tom said, "Wednesday is all-you-can-eat refried-beans day."

"Look, Tom, if you'll go somewhere else, I'll buy your lunch."

Without missing a beat, he said, "Okay. The food is not very good here anyway. Besides, it's really filthy.

Let's go get a nice, juicy steak."

One time Tom saw an ad in the newspaper. A local automotive store was having a sale on automobile batteries. The line that caught Tom's eye said, "40 percent off on some batteries."

Tom was there when they opened the next morning. He told the clerk that he needed a new battery.

"Boy, this is your lucky day," beamed the clerk. He started to show Tom the batteries. Tom said, "I'm interested in the ones that are forty percent off."

The clerk said, "Before you make up your mind, let me show you our top of the line, lifetime-guaranteed for seventy-five years, Super Duper Wizz-O Deluxe."

Tom said, "I'm really here to buy the one you advertised for forty percent off."

The clerk said, "Are you sure you want one of those?" When he said "one of those," he made a face like he had just taken a bite of liver.

Tom said, "Is anything wrong with it?"

"No, there is nothing wrong with it. Unless, of course, you want to do something like burn the lights or use your radio or heater."

Tom not only couldn't resist the bargain, he bought three of the sale batteries. "I saved 120 percent," he boasted.

When Tom got married, everybody in town knew that it could never last. The tongues wagged around the clock.

"Lord, Lord, how is poor Beth ever going to live with that skinflint? I bet you he still has the first penny he ever saw."

"Why, it's the truth. I do believe he's the worst nickel-nurser I ever did see."

Despite all the doom-sayers, the marriage seemed to be happy.

It was certainly not an average marriage. Tom, of course, handled all the money. He even did the grocery shopping. Deep down in his money-grubbing heart, he knew that if Beth ever got into a grocery store, she would buy something they didn't need, like paper towels or meat.

Tom and Beth were blessed with three sons—Tom Jr., Dennis and Michael.

It almost killed Tom when he found out that Tom Jr. had to have braces. He made Beth take him to four different orthodontists. It wasn't that he wanted four opinions; he wanted four estimates. The thought of putting $3,500 into a child's mouth was almost enough to turn his hair white.

He finally told Beth that he had decided not to buy the braces. When she demanded to know why, he told her that he felt like Tom Jr. would eventually outgrow his crooked teeth, but even if he didn't, it would be okay because he was so ugly anyway that nobody was going to look at his teeth.

He finally agreed to the braces when Beth threatened to leave him.

It was a proud day for the whole family when the dentist finally removed the braces from Tom Jr.'s mouth.

Beth was afraid she would spoil the festive occasion if she told Tom that while Tom Jr. was through with his braces, the dentist had told her that Michael needed braces and that the price had gone up to just over four thousand dollars.

When they finished dinner, she took Tom out of

earshot of the children and told him what the dentist had said. Tom's reply was almost predictable. He said, "No problem, we'll let him use Tom Jr.'s."

When Tom's father passed away, it fell Tom's lot to make all the funeral arrangements.

Tom and his daddy had never been real close, and Tom only had two thoughts about the funeral: Get it over with as quickly as possible and, of course, get it done for the absolute bottom dollar.

Tom was almost reduced to tears when the funeral director told him, in no uncertain terms, that it was against the law to bury his father in a wooden casket.

His penny-pinching reached new highs when he announced that he wanted to get three estimates before he made the final decision on a funeral home.

He haggled with the undertaker about almost everything, from the price of the coffin to whether or not he needed a hearse to get the dearly departed to the cemetery. After all, Tom said, he already owned a perfectly good pick-up truck.

Before the funeral was over, everybody in Tom's family was threatening to kill him and have a double funeral.

By the time Tom reached middle-age, he had made more enemies than Adolph Hitler.

When he died they searched high and low to get someone to do his eulogy. They were finally able to get our songwriter friend Lardo Dupree to say a few words in rhyme about old Tom.

The church for the funeral was not crowded. As a matter of fact, there were only eight people there, counting Tom. The widow was not even there. Someone said she had gone to Disney World.

When the preacher called on Lardo, he stood up, cleared his throat and said:

"Tom was tight, Tom was cheap, and there he lies, a lifeless heap. He was cheap in the summer, and cheap when it was snowin', and the Lord only knows where the cheap rascal's goin'. I'm not here to praise him, that's not why I'm here; besides, it's hot in this church, let's go have a beer."

Old Lardo had a way of cutting through the veneer.

Love Is Worth
The Price You Pay

LIKE MOST SIXTEEN-YEAR-old boys, Twilly had discovered sixteen-year-old girls, and believe me when I tell you that he was more excited about his discovery than Christopher Columbus ever was about his.

In the rural South of the 1930's, dates usually consisted of taking your girl to preachin' or just going to walk and holding hands. There was little else to do and little money to do it with.

In those Depression days, real dates were few and far between, and most of the social life between teen-aged boys and girls either took place at church or at school.

It was at school that Twilly met and fell madly in love with JudyRuth.

She was sixteen, beautiful, and she was just as attracted to Twilly as he was to her. The only fly in their ointment was JudyRuth's mother. She was a redheaded firebrand and believed by all to be the meanest woman in the world.

They owned a small dairy farm, and while her husband worked in the fields, she ran the dairy barn.

She always wore bib overalls and a flannel shirt. This fashion for women was unheard of in the 1930's.

Ludlow Porch

Mama also always carried a club, and many an uncooperative cow had been almost knocked to its knees by this less-than-genteel Amazon.

Once when she was asked about carrying a club, she replied, "A club upside the head is the only language most cows and some people understand."

One late summer afternoon, Twilly decided he would go calling on JudyRuth.

Walking down the dirt road to her house, he prayed out loud. "Dear Lord, please don't let her Mama be home, and if she is, please let her be in a good mood. Lord, you can forget about that last part. That woman ain't never been in a good mood."

Twilly walked up the stairs and across the front porch of the old farmhouse. All of his common sense and logic told him not to knock on that big front door. However, he wanted to see JudyRuth more than he was afraid of Mama and that club. Knowing better, he knocked on the door.

When the door opened, all of his worst fears were realized. Framed in the doorway was Mama looking as big as a house, and in her ham-like right hand was her club. It looked to Twilly like she was carrying a railroad crosstie. He was delighted that there was a screen door between them.

She looked down at him like he was a Republican cockroach and growled, "What do you want, white trash?"

"I'd like to see JudyRuth"

"Where do you know JudyRuth from, boy?"

"From school, ma'am."

"Well, you can't see her. She's got work to do, and even if she didn't, I don't want no kin of mine hanging out with cotton-mill trash like you. Now go on, boy, and don't let me catch you round her again. Gowon! Now, git!"

Knowing better than to argue with a crazy woman carrying a club, Twilly said, "Yes'em" and walked off the porch.

Twilly and JudyRuth continued to see each other at school, and sometimes while waiting for the school bus they would hold hands.

The worst day of Twilly's life started when the teacher said that right after lunch the whole school was going to the auditorium to see a movie about the three basic food groups.

Twilly didn't care about the three basic food groups, but he was excited because he knew that he was going to get to be with JudyRuth for forty-five minutes in a dark auditorium.

They met in the hall and went into the auditorium together. They sat as close to the back as they could. The lights had been out less than thirty seconds when they were holding hands.

Twilly thought to himself, I wonder if she would let me kiss her?

It took him about fifteen minutes to get up the necessary nerve. Then he got scared and nervous. What if she didn't let me? he thought. I would just die if she didn't want me to kiss her. What if someone saw us?

He thought of seventy-five reasons that he shouldn't kiss her, but on this day in that darkened auditorium, Cupid was not to be denied.

Slowly, Twilly slid his arm around JudyRuth's shoulder. When she turned toward him, he gave her a ten-second kiss. To his delight, she kissed back.

He was so pleased at her reaction that he put his other arm around her and really planted one on her.

He was so full of the moment that he didn't realize at first what was happening as Mr. Whitley, the principal, dragged them both out of their seats and was pushing them down the aisle toward the hall.

Once in the hall, Mr. Whitley said in a loud sarcastic voice, "Just what do you two sex fiends think you are doing?"

Looking at the floor, Twilly said, "Nuthin."

"Nothing? Nothing? You call that nothing, boy? If that's nothing, I'd sure hate to see you doing something. Don't deny it. I saw you plain as anything. You kissed that girl full on the mouth, and the disgraceful part is she was kissing you back.

"You two may think that raw sex in the auditorium is okay, but before I get through with you, you'll realize that Christian conduct is not kissing on the mouth in my auditorium."

He hauled the two terrified teen-agers into his office and continued to lecture them for the better part of an hour. He didn't let them out of the office until he gave each one a note to their parents giving all the details of the kissing episode, as he called it.

He finally dismissed them by saying, "You bring those notes back tomorrow, signed by your parents. I'll decide by then what I'm going to do to you. Now, get out of my sight, you two perverts."

When Twilly got home, he took the note straight to his mother. She said, "Well, you shouldn't have done it, but I reckon if kissin' was a sin, there wouldn't be enough folks in heaven to get up a good checker game."

He was relieved by his mother's reaction, but he was also convinced that JudyRuth's mama was not going to be that understanding.

He didn't sleep well that night, for fear of the unknown will keep you awake every time.

When he got to school the next morning, his teacher told him that he was to go straight to the principal's office. When he went into the office, his blood turned immediately to ice. There stood the last person on earth he wanted to see—JudyRuth's great big old red-headed mama.

Mr. Whitley, obviously enjoying the terror in Twilly's face, said, "Sit down. I believe JudyRuth's mother has something to say to you."

Mama said, "This won't take long, Mr. Whitley." Then turning to the trembling Twilly, she said, "Trash, I done told you once to stay away from that girl and you didn't do it. Well, young man, let me tell you that if I ever even hear about you speaking one syllable to her, I'm going to tear off your arm and beat you to death with the bloody stump.

"You ain't nothin' but gutter dirt, boy, and nothin' would give me any greater pleasure than to rid the earth of white trash like you. You let me catch you moping around my girl, and I'll tear off your lips and mail 'em to your mama. Do you have any questions, white trash?"

"No ma'am."

"Good, 'cause if I have to kill you, it'll be suicide and not murder."

With those parting words of wisdom, she pushed Twilly out of the way and stomped out of the office.

To say she made an impression on Twilly would be

like saying the Pacific Ocean is moist.

The first week there was no contact between Twilly and JudyRuth. They both knew that Mr. Whitley had people watching them, and they also knew that nothing would have given him more pleasure than to catch them talking or doing anything else, for that matter. When they would meet in the hall, they would even avoid eye contact.

The rekindling of their romance started slowly. One day Twilly picked up his geography book and found a note written on Blue Horse notebook paper. The note said, "JudyRuth loves Twilly, XXXXXX."

When Twilly saw the note, his heart jumped right up between his ears. He immediately wrote his own love note. It said, "The kiss was worth it. I love you."

When they passed in the hall, he slipped the love note into her hand. It was a big chance to take, but he had to let her know that redheaded mama or no redheaded mama, she was his girl.

The notes became more frequent, sometimes as many as three or four a day. Toward the end of the second week, he found a note that read, "I can slip out of the house tonight. Please meet me in the road, a hundred yards from my house at midnight. I love you."

Twilly was so happy and excited that he had to go to the boys' bathroom and throw up. He couldn't think about anything else for the rest of the day.

When he got home from school, he went about his chores and then went straight to his homework.

During dinner his mother said, "Twilly, do you feel all right?"

He said, "Sure do. Why do you ask?"

"Well, you just picked at your dinner and besides,

you ain't quit smiling since you got off that school bus."

He assured her that he was in perfect health.

Twilly went to bed at the usual time, but he took only his shoes off. He laid there in bed waiting for the hands on his Big Ben alarm clock to tell him when it was time to go meet the love of his sixteen-year-old life, the wonderful JudyRuth.

He figured it would take him thirty minutes to walk to their meeting place. When the clock finally said eleven, he very quietly eased out of bed, picked his shoes up and slowly, ever so slowly, raised the window. He dropped to the ground.

He didn't stop to put his shoes on until he was well down the road from his house.

He had no sense of danger as he walked toward the rendezvous. Why should he worry? If JudyRuth had the nerve, why shouldn't he? He knew that her mama got up every morning at 5 A.M. to do the milkin' and that because of that she had been in bed sound asleep for hours. The thought of any chance of being caught quickly left his mind as he arrived at the appointed spot.

His heart stopped when he realized that she was not there. He walked a little further up the road but still no JudyRuth.

The moon finally came out from behind a cloud and down the road he saw her coming toward him.

It was a lovely, tender moment. They were there in the middle of that dirt road, hugging and kissing.

The first time he noticed any danger was when he heard a voice yell, "I told you I'd kill you, trash, and kill you I will."

Twilly had been so involved with his huggin' and

kissin' that she was within about three feet of him before he saw her. She swung the club and missed Twilly's left ear by about two inches.

Twilly turned and started to sprint down that dirt road like his life was in danger, which, as a matter of fact, it was.

He was sure that he could outrun her and was therefore a little surprised when he looked back and saw that not only was she gaining on him, but she did not seem to be breathing hard.

Every step she took she was screaming threats at the wide-open Twilly. "You'd better run, you low-life cotton-mill trash, 'cause when I catch you, I'm gonna bash your dirty brains all over this road."

Twilly toyed with the idea of trying to outrun her all the way to his house, but he instantly realized that as mad as she was, she probably would follow him in and beat him to death in his own home.

He decided that his best bet for survival was just to run.

He was, of course, much younger than her, and how far could that crazy woman run carrying a thirty-pound club?

He looked over his shoulder again and, to his horror, realized that she actually seemed to be gaining on him.

It was time for some drastic action. If he could not outrun her, he would try to outsmart her.

They were just passing Mr. Luther Boyd's house. His cornfield was planted right beside the house. Twilly reasoned that if he could make it to the cornfield, he could lose his attacker and thereby live to see another sunrise.

He cut quickly to the right and in about four long

strides was in the cornfield, running over cornstalks till hell wouldn't have it.

What neither Twilly nor his would-be assassin knew was that there was somebody else in that cornfield. Mr. Boyd had received a call from Mother Nature in the middle of the night and had elected to go to the cornfield rather than the further distance to his outhouse.

There he was squatting in his own cornfield, overalls around his ankles, at full peace with God and man.

It was at this moment that JudyRuth's mama spotted him squatting there. She, of course, assumed that it was Twilly trying to hide from her.

The first time Mr. Boyd knew he was not alone was when he looked up and saw her coming toward him with the club over her head screaming, "I got you now, you oversexed sumbitch. Get ready to meet your maker." She beat him till he lost consciousness and left him lying there alone, bleeding and with his overalls still around his ankles.

Several days later, Mr. Boyd went into the barber shop. Twilly was there waiting to get a haircut. Mr. Boyd was a mess. He had two black eyes, a tooth missing right in the front and a place on the top of his head that was shaved so the doctor could take some stitches.

"What in the name of God happened to you, Luther?" asked Sam, the barber.

He repeated the whole story while everybody in the barber shop except Twilly tried not to laugh.

When he got through with his story, Sam asked, "Who do you reckon it was, Luther?"

Luther said, "It wasn't a who, it was a what. It was a monster, I tell you. It had four arms, and every one was swinging a club. I don't know what it was, but it was from another planet, I'll guarantee you that."

Thus was born the legend of Luther Boyd's cornfield creature.

Sam said, "Well, Luther, what do you aim to do about it?"

Luther said, "I've already done it. The plumber's out to my house right now putting in an indoor toilet."

I guess all's well that ends well, because about three years later, Twilly and JudyRuth ran off and got married and, as they say, lived happily everafter.

The only disappointing thing was that the mystery of the cornfield creature was never solved.

Charlie Walked Too Close to the Edge

I GUESS THERE'S A difference between being accident-prone and being dumb, but I've never been exactly sure what it was.

I haven't made any official study of either dumb people or accident-prone people, but I know a lot of folks in both groups and one conclusion is inescapable: While all dumb people are not accident-prone, it seems to be that all accident-prone people are dumb.

Charlie was dumb. He made a nice appearance and had a pleasant personality, but he was dumb.

Let me prove my point about Charlie's intelligence quotient with a couple of examples:

Did you ever hear of anyone being bitten by a copperhead while tying a string around the snake's neck?

Did you ever hear of anyone nailing their thumb to a wall while hanging a picture?

These trips into lunacy were only two of the freak accidents and injuries that have been a part of Charlie's life, man and boy.

Charlie's trip toward self-destruction started at a very early age. When he was about ten he began begging his mother for a bicycle. She discussed it in great detail with Charlie's daddy. All the other boys had bicycles, and it's hard to explain to a ten-year-old that buying him a bicycle will almost certainly lead to massive injuries.

Charlie's daddy said, "Ethyl, you know we can't get that boy a bike. My God, woman! Don't you remember last year when he broke his arm changing the channel on the television?"

They were able to stall young Charlie until his twelfth birthday when, against their better judgment, they bought him a bike.

It was a beauty — a "Western Flyer" and the very best that the Western Auto Store had to offer. It had a basket on the front so that Charlie could go pick up groceries for his mama. It had a horn and a solid-chrome luggage rack. In short, it was about the prettiest bike anybody ever owned.

Charlie was so happy that he couldn't wait for his friends to see it. He got on the phone almost at once, telling everybody he knew about his "new wheel."

But the new bike was like everything else in Charlie's life. It soon proved to be a problem.

Charlie could ride the bike well enough, but he had a great deal of trouble stopping it. He could not bring himself to put on the brakes. He said it was scary. It seemed crazy to me, but then most of the things Charlie did seemed crazy to me.

His approach to this problem was much like his approach to life — he hit it head on. When Charlie was ready to stop his bike, he ran into whatever was handy.

He preferred thick hedge bushes because they wouldn't damage his priceless bicycle. However, it soon became apparent even to Charlie that sometimes you can't find a hedge when you need one. On those occasions he just did the best he could. He would ride into a dirt bank or a tree or whatever obstruction happened to be handy. By the time the bike was ten days old, it looked like it had spent a good deal of time in a trash compactor.

The end to Charlie's bike came on a beautiful Saturday afternoon.

The neighborhood was empty of kids. Everyone had gone to the Fairfax theatre for a double feature — Charlie Chan in *The Trembling Chiropractor* and Johnny Mack Brown in *Six-gun Symphony*. Since there was no one to play with, Charlie decided to ride his bike. But with no one to ride with him, that soon got dull, so he decided to see how far he could ride with his eyes closed.

The ride proved to be a further extension of Charlie's march toward self-destruction. He was only about forty yards down Spring Street when his adventure came to a predictable halt. He was treated at the hospital for a broken right leg and a severe dog bite.

He had been peddling like crazy when Mr. Reynold's favorite bird dog, Red, had crossed in front of him. Charlie wasn't hurt in the bike wreck, but Red took a bite out of him while they were tangled up, and when Mr. Reynolds saw what Charlie had done, he broke his leg.

On Charlie's sixteenth birthday, he totaled out his father's car. This would, in itself, not be too unusual. A lot of sixteen-year-olds total out cars.

Charlie, however, was taking the test for his driver's license at the time of the wreck.

When he turned eighteen, he saw John Wayne in a

movie about the Marine Corps. He decided that since John Wayne seemed to be having so much fun, he would join the Marines.

When his mother found out, she almost had a running fit. Charlie's father took a different approach. He told his wife, "Mama, that boy has had a death wish since he was eighteen months old. He might as well do it where they got free medical care. Besides, I'm getting tired of spending all my leisure time in a hospital waiting room."

Charlie's military career lasted exactly forty-seven days. On the rifle range at Parris Island, he shot himself in the foot and received a medical discharge.

In the next few years, Charlie bounced from job to job and from injury to injury.

I had not heard from Charlie for quite sometime until one day he called me. He was absolutely bubbling over. He said, "You ain't gonna believe this, man, but for the first time in my life, I just won something."

I naturally asked, "How?"

He said, "I just won first prize on a radio contest, and all I had to do was mail in one post card."

I said, "Charlie, that's great. What did you win?"

Still bubbling, he said, "An all-expense-paid, two-week fishing vacation in the Pacific northwest."

"Lucky stiff! Where in the Pacific northwest?"

He said, "I ain't exactly sure. It's a place called Mount St. Helen's."

I haven't heard from old Charlie since. I wonder if he caught any fish?

Montana Is Right For Mr. Macho

WHEN I CONSIDERED WRITING about a macho man, I tried to think of someone I knew or knew about who would be a perfect model. I soon decided, however, that it would be impossible to write about *one* person who was macho.

My research served to show that macho means different things to different people. What is considered macho to one might be considered white trash to another.

The best definition I came up with was: "A macho man is someone who would jog home from his vasectomy."

In defining the macho man, it is not enough to know what he is. It is just as important to know what he is *not*.

For example, a macho man would never have a tattoo that said "Mother." His tattoo would say "Death Before Dishonor."

He would never go to the ballet, much preferring a tractor pull or a cockfight.

He doesn't worry a great deal about his vocabulary because he is safe in the knowledge that all he has to do to be macho is never say more than three sentences without the word *shit* being used in some manner.

He would never wear a suit with a vest, preferring instead some sort of cowboy attire.

He would never own a cat or a small dog, favoring instead large dogs, such as dobermans or German shepherds. In some cases macho men also own boa constrictors. That qualifies as ultra macho.

They refer to their wives as "my old lady."

They refer to all other women as "broads."

The real macho man does not care much for children but feels compelled to be a little-league coach.

In the 1960's, a new type of macho man was born. He was inspired by the James Bond movies. Suddenly new macho was in. That meant no more Pabst Blue Ribbon. It suddenly meant that to be macho you had to order only exotic or exotic-sounding drinks.

A vodka martini, stirred, not shaken, or a Pink Rob Roy.

It meant that you had to wear driving gloves and enjoy raw fish.

You had to know some foreign words like *ciao*.

You had to be into scuba diving and, most importantly, you had to jog. No macho man worth his salt in the eighties would be a non-jogger.

Lest it sound like I am anti-macho man, let me explain that nothing could be further from the truth. I like them just fine. I particularly like them in Montana and me in Georgia.

The Napalm Crew Was a Handful

I'M NOT SURE HOW the hatred between the Marine Corps and the Navy started. I've heard that it started because the Navy hospital corpsmen seemed to take such great pleasure in giving shots with those square, dull needles. Or perhaps it was because Marines are always guards at Navy brigs.

No matter how it started, it's real and it goes on till this day. Sailors refer to Marines as "jarheads," "jungle bunnies," and "bellhops." Marines refer to sailors as "deck apes," "squids," "swabbies" and "rust pickers."

I don't know about the Navy, but Marines are almost required to hate sailors.

It starts at boot camp when the D.I. announces in a loud voice, through clenched teeth (come to think of it, everything he said was in a loud voice through clenched teeth), "I don't want you burr-headed idiots going on sick call. You know why? I'll tell you why. 'Cause there ain't nobody working in that sickbay except sailors, and we don't want to ask them rust-pickin', pill-pushin' faggots for nothin'."

On liberty on any given evening, you can always

either hear about or actually see a Marine and a sailor in a fist-fight.

When you're eighteen years old, away from home for the first time and in the Marines, punching a sailor in the mouth doesn't seem like such a bad thing to do. As a matter of fact, it seems to be part of the natural order of things.

In April 1952, Marine Air Group 24 was sent to Roosevelt Roads, Puerto Rico, on maneuvers. It was called "Operation Traex." That's Marine Corps language for training exercise.

Roosevelt Roads is a naval base. It's not much of a naval base, but that's what the government calls it, so I guess that makes it official.

As an eighteen-year-old Marine, I felt that "Operation Traex" would be a great adventure. Besides, the name Roosevelt Roads sounded like a nice place to be. I was, however, mistaken.

The sailors lived at the base in their white barracks. The Marines lived in tents in the jungle, eating C-rations, and fighting mosquitoes as big as crows.

The nearest town was about twenty miles away, and as bad as it was, it beat the jungle. We lived for the rare times we were allowed to go on liberty.

In 1952 "Rosey Roads," as it was called, was a small, remote base, so small, in fact, that neither the Navy nor the Marines had regular M.P.'s or S.P.'s stationed there.

One weekend the Navy furnished the shore patrol in town, and the next week the Marines pulled the M.P. duty.

Since we didn't have any regular M.P.'s, they picked us at random to put on an armband, take a night stick and patrol the streets in that small liberty town.

The Napalm Crew Was a Handful

The first time I caught M.P. duty, the NCOIC (Non-commissioned Officer in Charge) was a master sargeant that we affectionately called "Screamin' Nick." His real name was Nick Webb. He had been in the Corps for eighteen years. He was about 5'10" tall and built like a wedge.

Pound for pound, Screamin' Nick was meaner than a Bengal tiger. He screamed every word. I never heard him speak in a normal tone of voice. To say he hated sailors would be like saying King Tut was dead. He despised and loathed everything even remotely connected to the Navy.

Ten of us, not counting Sgt. Webb, were assigned to the M.P.'s. They issued our armbands and night sticks and, prior to loading us on trucks for the bumpy ride into town, Sgt. Webb had us fall in for inspection.

He walked up and down, checking us one by one for starched uniforms and shined shoes. When he was satisfied that we were squared away, he started his little speech.

"Men," he bellowed, "here are your orders for the night. You are to patrol the streets in pairs and make sure that all the Marines in town are squared away and not too drunk to walk and talk and act like Marines.

"Order No. 2 is to arrest all sailors, tall or short, drunk or sober. I want every one of them rust pickers arrested by midnight. Any questions?"

"Arrest them for what, Sgt. Webb?"

"Boy! You don't need a reason to arrest a deck ape! You just arrest them for the hell of it. Besides, they ain't fit to be in the same town with real fighting men."

We walked down the street until we came to the first bar. We stopped at the door and Sgt. Webb said,

"Remember, every sailor in there is drunk and disorderly. Now, go do your duty."

It goes without saying that they were neither drunk nor disorderly. They had only been in town about thirty minutes, and they had no intention of being arrested.

The fight lasted about ten minutes, but when it was over, there were no white hats to be seen. Before the night was over, not a single sailor was left on the street.

The next night the Navy had the shore patrol duty, and, of course, they went into town and immediately arrested all the Marines.

Both factions fumed all week long and everyone at "Rosey Roads" wondered who would surrender first and if the *espirit de corps* could hold out for another weekend.

Friday night came and, sure enough, all the sailors who had dared to go to town were arrested.

Saturday night was to be the big showdown. Both sides knew it was only a matter of time before the civilian authorities complained to the brass about the regularly scheduled riots that were being held in the streets of their little town.

It was at this point that the Napalm Crew decided to take matters into their own hands.

The Napalm Crew consisted of eight Marines. Their job for "Operation Traex" was to assemble the napalm tanks, mix the napalm and hang the full tank on the airplane. It was not a particularly difficult thing to do, but these eight men were the only people who knew how to do it. The undisputed leader of the Napalm Crew was a corporal named Brock from Spartanburg, South Carolina.

Brock had been in the Corps longer than the others

and therefore hated sailors more than they did. He was only twenty-two years old and the oldest member of this rowdy bunch. PFC Owens was Brock's best friend. Owens was seventeen or eighteen years old. He was about six-feet tall and weighed about 160 pounds. He was a right nice guy but seemed to like fist-fighting the way we liked volleyball.

The Napalm Crew arrived in town on the first bus and made their way to a little tiny bar. Once inside, Brock made his announcement.

"Ain't no sailor arresting me tonight. If we stick together, we can handle them rust-pickin' bastards."

It was agreed among them that under no circumstances would they allow themselves to be placed under arrest. It didn't take long for their resolve to be tested.

Two S.P.'s showed the bad judgment to go into the bar alone. Their attempt to arrest the eight members of the Napalm Crew turned out to be a serious error.

The Napalm Crew took their nightsticks and armbands away from them and threw the S.P.'s through a large wooden door.

They all had a good laugh and tried to calm the bartender, who was near tears.

They were all leaning against the bar savoring their victory when Owens turned to Brock and asked, "Do you think they'll be back with reenforcements?"

Brock smiled and said, "Unless I miss my guess, in a few minutes we're gonna be up to our skivvies in sailors."

Brock, however, was not expecting what happened next.

One of the sailors that they had thrown through the

door got on the telephone and called the base. The Navy C.O. apparently decided it was time to halt this foolishness once and for all, and he sent every available sailor to put down the open rebellion of the Napalm Crew.

None of the young Marines was worried about going to the brig. After all, they were the Napalm Crew. If they were locked up, there was no one to mix the napalm, and the entire exercise would come to a halt.

When the sailors started to arrive in town, it looked like a convoy. They came in staff cars, jeeps, a wrecker and two pick-up trucks. They also brought a semi to haul their prisoners back to the brig in.

The fight that took place in that tiny bar made the Battle of Midway pale in comparison.

It took about thirty minutes to get all the Marines out of the bar and locked safely in the trailor of the semi. On the way back to the base, the semi laden with its prisoners led the convoy.

Meanwhile, Brock and Owens and their six angry friends were plotting their next move.

Brock said, "Only one thing to do when we get to the brig. When they unlock that door, we all jump out at once and start taking names and kicking ass."

They all agreed that this was a wonderful plan.

They arrived at the brig with the convoy following. When the poor, unsuspecting sailor unlocked the door, the Napalm Crew all hit the ground at one time. They started back to the other cars, pulling sailors out as they went.

Soon the riot was back on, and it took another thirty minutes to get them all inside the brig and into cells.

They were a sad sight when the sun came up — torn

clothes, dried blood and bruised faces.

Owens was still wearing a sailor hat and a S.P. arm-band.

The rum and beer they had consumed had produced eight separate but equal hangovers.

What had seemed like a good idea to them the night before now struck them as foolish, except for Brock. He was still a little drunk and shouting insults at the Navy guards.

The brig warden came in and opened the cells. "Okay, jarheads, fall in outside," he growled.

They walked outside in their ragged uniforms, and there stood Sgt. Webb and their Capt. Southern.

Screamin' Nick, obviously trying to impress the Captain, said, "Okay, idiots, fall in and try to act like Marines."

He screamed at them nonstop for ten minutes. The captain watched in silent disgust. Finally, Sgt. Webb stopped in front of Brock, who was standing at attention, one sleeve missing from his shirt and huge tears running down his cheeks.

Webb screamed at the drunk Brock, "Why are you crying, Brock? You look like an idiot."

Blubbering now, Brock said, "Ya should have seen it, Sargeant. It was beautiful."

"What was beautiful?"

Still crying, Brock said, "It took three sailors to put Owens in his cell, and he took two of them in with him."

The entire Napalm Crew was restricted to the base for two weeks, but no further action was taken against them.

The Navy brig warden filed a formal protest because

they had wrecked his brig, beat up his sailors, and no one had been court-martialed or even busted in rank.

The Napalm Crew was as amazed as the Navy that they had not been executed. It took them three months to find out who their benefactor was.

One day, during inspection, Screamin' Nick stepped in front of the ramrod-straight Owens.

In a very low voice, he said, "Owens, do you remember being in that brig down at 'Rosey Roads'?"

"Yes, sir."

"How many deck apes did it take to put you in that cell?"

"Three, sir."

"And how many did you take in with you, Owens?"

"Two, sir."

At that moment something happened that we had never seen before. Sgt. "Screamin' Nick" Webb smiled a huge smile and said in a very soft, loving, almost fatherly tone, "You're a hell of a Marine, Owens. Yes, sir, one hell of a Marine."

Are You Sure You're Not Sick?

MORE STRANGE THINGS GO on in hospitals than any other place in the world. I suspect one reason for that is that hospital employees do many things out of tradition rather than reason.

For example, hospital workers have a preoccupation with the bladder and the bowel habits of their customers. I'm not by nature an overly private person, but I do believe that my bladder and bowel habits are between me and my creator.

I went into a hospital once to visit a friend. The information desk was manned by a retired nurse.

I said, "What room is Mr. Garner in?"

She said, "He's in Room 312. When did you have your last bowel movement?"

"I beg your pardon?"

"Sorry," she said. "Force of habit."

Even when you check into a hospital for something minor, like a simple physical exam or an x-ray, the strangeness starts and doesn't stop until you are discharged.

The first thing they do is take all your clothes away from you. I don't mean some of your clothes, I mean they take every stitch. I've never been able to figure it out, but for some reason known only to that hospital staff, they want you in there naked.

I believe that when you're staying in a place that costs four hundred dollars a day, the very least you could expect, after they've taken all your clothes, is that they will furnish you with a nice pair of pajamas.

You can forget that. They give you a little old night gown that if you're lucky will come down to about your knees.

If you're not lucky, you're going to find out what they mean by I.C.U. unit.

Once they get you in that twenty-nine cent night-gown, I don't understand why they didn't spend another dime and put a zipper up the back. Instead, they have little ties about every ten inches, and the back of the gown seems to gap open from top to bottom. It is beyond the shadow of a doubt the most immodest thing a human being, male or female, can wear. You can feel the breeze, and you're afraid to let anybody stand behind you because you're not really sure what's showing.

The sun comes up early in a hospital, and when you're there for tests, you usually get a delightful breakfast of air-flavored Jello, warm skimmed milk, cold, unbuttered toast and at least one unrecognizable dish. Then when they pick up your breakfast tray a nurse says, "You didn't eat your wonderful breakfast."

I usually answer, "You must have given the wonderful breakfast to someone else, because I got the Jello."

Finally they come and get you for your x-rays. You don't want to get out of the bed because of that gown with the gapped open back, and you're still not sure what's showing.

They finally get you down into the x-ray department. There they bring out a marble table that they've been keeping in the refrigerator for about three months. The minute you get on that table, you know exactly what's been showing since you've been there.

Then the x-ray technician comes in. She is usually a young lady in a fresh white uniform. She checks to make sure you're uncomfortable, then she starts to pull this huge piece of equipment across the floor over your head. It looks like something out of a science fiction movie.

You're paying big money for the right to be there, so you have a right to ask questions. Sheepishly, you say, "Excuse me, dear heart, but that looks dangerous. What is it?"

This angel of mercy, this healer of mankind, stops what she's doing, looks at you like your were a cockroach and says, "Don't be a gutless coward, fatso. This is a harmless x-ray machine. It is a great tool of medical science and there is no way on earth that it can hurt you. Now, stop your whinning."

Then she goes and gets behind a solid lead shield to turn it on.

From Dr. Kildare to Ben Casey to General Hospital, television and the movies have always glamorized hospitals.

Have you ever noticed on those shows how the patient is in a bed made up with fresh white sheets and a little buzzer pinned to the pillow?

On TV if the patient needs anything from a drink of

water to a bath, all he has to do is pick up the buzzer, press the button and in about three and one-half seconds the door swings open and in rush five doctors and twelve nurses, ready to take care of the patient's every need.

The last time I was in the hospital, I mashed that little old buzzer until the lights went dim in the operating room. The first human being I saw was three hours later when a very nice Puerto Rican man came in to talk about my insurance.

When I assured him I was in good hands, he laughed loudly. I started looking for my clothes.

Hospitals are great places and, Lord knows, they perform miracles every day. But if you're into strangeness, just go sit around in the lobby. It's always good for a few laughs.

The Norm Is Not Normal in N.Y.

IF YOU TRULY ENJOY the fine art of weirdo watching, New York City is the place to spend your next vacation.

New Yorkers you meet on a one-to-one social basis are pretty much like people everywhere, but as a group they spend most of their time either trying to get through traffic or to avoid standing in a line. That lifestyle requires that they be a little weird just to survive.

The last trip I made to the Big Apple was one of those up-and-back-on-the-same-day business trips. I got off the airplane and made my way out to the ground transportation area to catch a cab.

The first thing I saw was a burly taxi driver and an equally burly taxi dispatcher in a fist fight over thirty-five cents. The air around them was blue as a result of some of the language they were using. They both had bloody noses and their shirts were torn.

The thing that struck me as weird was there were about five hundred people walking up and down the street and none of them seemed to notice that a bloody fist-fight was in progress.

A blue-uniformed policeman finally noticed what

was happening and strolled up to the two fighters. Never raising his voice over a normal conversational tone, he said something that sounded like, "Aaa! Aaa! Wasamatteryoutwo? Youcrazy or somethin? Knockit off foreIrunyoursebotin."

They seemed to understand his strange language because they stopped throwing punches, but they continued to shout insults at each other.

The cop became visibily irritated at this point and yelled in a loud voice, "Itoldyousebottoknockitoff. Nowknockitoffor I'llcrack yaskull."

I don't handle this kind of open hostility well, so as I stood there watching a thought suddenly hit me: I wonder if Delta is *really* ready when I am. It was at that moment that the assistant dispatcher ushered me into a waiting cab.

I was relieved to have all this craziness out of my life. I was going downtown to take care of my business and hopefully be out of there before dark. I felt pretty good about this until I looked up and saw a sign on the back of the front seat. It read, "Driver will change no bill larger than a ten."

My blood ran a few degrees cooler when I realized that only seconds before I had seen two grown men in a bloody fist-fight over thirty-five cents, and now the smallest bill I had on me was a twenty.

I immediately hit on a plan. I thought to myself, I'll be so friendly and so Southern that by the time we get downtown, my driver will like me so much that he'll drop me off by a Seven-Eleven and let me get my twenty-dollar bill changed.

I thought my plan was foolproof. I remembered the words of some long-dead wise person who said, "You can catch more flies with honey than with vinegar."

With my plan firmly in mind, I sat back in the seat, loosened my tie and said in my friendliest voice, "I need to go to 500 Park Avenue. Do you know where that is?"

My driver never looked around. Still facing the front he said, "Jas."

I said, "It sure is a beautiful day, ain't it?"

My driver said, "Jas."

"How do you think the Mets are going to do this year?" I asked.

My driver answered, "Jas."

I said to myself, "Oh, hell! Here I am seven hundred miles from the nearest glass of buttermilk, stuck in a taxi cab with the Cisco Kid, and he's not even going to know why he's cuttin' me."

I have a theory that has been with me since childhood. I think the Good Lord looks after Southerners when they're north of Richmond, Virginia. My theory held up, 'cause at that very moment we passed a large sign on the side of the expressway that said, "Toll booth five hundred feet ahead."

I said, "Thank you, Jesus." Then I tapped my driver on the shoulder and said, "I'll pay the toll".

My driver said, "Jas."

I really felt that my troubles were over, but that good feeling didn't last too long, 'cause at about that time the biggest, meanest-looking man I had ever seen in my life came lumbering out of that toll booth. He was about 6'9" and looked like he weighed in at about 340 lbs.

He looked somewhat like a muscular Arnold Schwartzenagger.

He was wearing a dingy yellow tank top, and all the skin showing had hair on it. On the front of his yellow tank top it said, "I hate earthlings." He had one eyebrow that went all the way across his forehead.

As he approached the taxi, I noticed that he didn't have tattoos . . . he had iron-on transfers.

I sheepishly stuck my twenty-dollar bill out of the back window of the taxi. When he recognized it as a twenty, you could feel that giant body go suddenly tight.

Then he started to talk in a breathy voice that sounded a little like Clint Eastwood. He said, "I knew it, I just knew it. If you stand here long enough, sooner or later some idiot is going to come through here with nothing but a big bill and take all of your change." His voice was growing louder with each word. He went on, "Nothing on God's earth makes me any madder than to have some clown come through here and take all of my change, knowing full well that I've got no other way to get change and that I've got to stand here all day and argue with surly New York commuters because some imbecile only had a twenty-dollar bill."

His voice growing still louder, he said, "Someday that's going to happen to me and I'm going to reach in the back seat of a taxi and tear somebody's damn throat out." He leaned over so he could see me better and growled, "Is that the smallest bill you got, *fella*?"

I said, "Jas." You could see the hate increase in his eyes as he snatched the twenty out of my hand and disappeared back into the toll booth. I could hear him in there kicking things, making change and cussing Puerto Ricans.

In about thirty seconds he came storming out of the

toll booth, still grumbling, and threw a handful of one dollar bills in the back window of the taxi.

I couldn't stand it any longer. As the taxi pulled away from the toll booth, I hung my head out of the window and yelled back at my tormentor, "Ya'll come to see us, ya heah?"

You could tell by the look on my taxi driver's face that he did not know why I was lying down on the seat laughing wildly. It was not that I thought it was so funny, but I did consider it one of life's little victories.

When I reached my destination, I paid my nearly mute driver and said, "Thanks a lot."

He said, "Jas."

I walked into the office building where my appointment was, checked the lobby directory and pushed the up button on the elevator.

There was a neatly dressed man standing beside me also waiting for the elevator. When our eyes met, I smiled and said, "Good morning."

He returned my smile and said, "I've decided not to go to Reno."

"I beg your pardon?"

He said, "I don't know how to say it any plainer than that. I told you that I've decided not to go to Reno."

A little confused, I said, "Oh, really?"

"Is that all you have to say, 'Oh, really'? I've just told you that I'm not going to Reno and you just stand there and say, 'Oh, really?' " Then in a very irritated voice, he added, "You don't really care, do you? Go ahead, admit it. You don't care if I go to Reno or not. Tell the truth, you don't really care, do you?"

Suddenly my white-trash background came out. I said, "Ace, I'm gonna level with you. Not only do I not care if you go to Reno, I don't give a rat's ass if you live or die, and if you don't stop yelling at me, I'm gonna knock your nose in your watch pocket."

He paused, only a moment, and said, "Did you know my kid sister was once married to John the Baptist?"

I said, "Oh, really?"

He started to shout, "There you go with that 'Oh, really' crap again. You don't believe me, do you? I'm sick of you and your negative attitude. Don't move. I'm going to get my cousin, Zorro, and he's going to challenge you to a duel. You'll see, don't move. I'll be right back with my cousin Zorro. Don't move," he ordered, and he stormed off across the lobby of the building yelling. "Zorro will fix your ass, you'll see."

I was happier than usual to see the elevator door open.

My business meeting lasted longer than planned, and it soon became obvious that I was going to have to stay overnight in New York and finish my business the following day.

I reluctantly checked into a nearby hotel. It was a rather nice place, and I remember thinking to myself, This is not going to be so bad. I'll just sit in my room, enjoy a little TV, take a shower and get a good night's sleep.

I was just getting interested in the television when there was a knock on my door. I looked out of the peephole and saw two men in uniforms that I could not identify. I opened the door and one of them said, "We're the exterminators."

"Are you kidding?" I said. "It's 7:30 at night."

The man said, "Cockroaches ain't got no watches."

"How long will it take?"

The more intelligent of the two said, "Ten minutes, tops."

"Are you sure this is necessary?"

"What do you mean, necessary? We got cockroaches in here as big as alley cats."

I said, "Did you ever do any PR work?"

"Look, are you gonna let us in or not?"

"I still don't believe this is happening," I said, "but come on in so we can get this over with."

They came in, both carrying little chrome tanks with spray nozzles attached. They sprayed all the base boards, then they opened all the drawers and sprayed inside.

When they were about three-quarters finished, one turned to me and said, "Sure does stink, don't it?"

I said, "Boy, you can say that again. How long before the odor goes away?"

"All you have to do is open the windows, and in three or four hours you'll never know we were here."

"Are you serious? Three or four hours? I was planning on going to bed."

He said, "Suit yourself, but if you go to bed without airing this place out, you'll be taking your life in your own hands. Why don't you go downstairs to our restaurant, have a nice dinner, three or four drinks and by the time you get back the smell will be all gone."

I turned to the other guy and said, "Is that right?"

He looked at me and said, "Why don't you go downstairs to our restaurant, have a nice dinner, three or four drinks and by the time you get back the smell will be all gone."

"Is there an echo in here?" I asked.

The first guy said, "I don't think so, why?"

Ludlow Porch

The second guy said, "I don't think so, why?"

"Never mind. I think I'll go downstairs to your restaurant, have a nice dinner, three or four drinks and by the time I get back the smell will be all gone."

They both nodded and I left the room and headed for the restaurant downstairs.

I had a shrimp cocktail, steak and the rest of what turned out to be a pretty good meal. I looked at my watch. I had been out of the room for only one hour and fifteen minutes. I paid my tab and asked directions to the lounge.

There were no tables available, so I spotted an empty seat at the bar and squeezed in between two other men who seemed to be as bored as I was.

I struck up a conversation with the man sitting to my left. When he found out I was from Atlanta, he seemed delighted. He said he had been in the Army at Ft. Benning, Georgia, and had many happy memories of pleasant weekends in Atlanta.

We talked on for about an hour and finally I asked him what his job was in the Army.

I was surprised when he told me that he had been a chaplain. I smiled and said, "I would never have guessed that you were a preacher."

He laughed and said, "No, actually, I was a Catholic priest."

"That's very interesting. Where's your church?"

"Oh, I'm not a priest anymore," he said. "I've been defrocked."

Trying to be sympathetic, I said, "I'm sorry."

"Oh, I'm over it now. You see, they threw me out when they found out my true identity."

"Your true identity?" I asked.

156

He went on, obviously enjoying himself. "Yes, they just couldn't handle it when they found out I was actually Robin Hood. That business with Maid Marion, you know. But I think the thing that really hacked the Pope off was when they found out I wasn't Catholic. They really prefer that all their priests be Catholic. You know, I'm not sure, but I think it goes all the way back to Pat O'Brien."

I said, "Hey, nice talking to you, but I think I better turn in." I figured I was safer with the bug spray.

"Don't rush off," he said. "The Sheriff of Nottingham is due any minute and I'm going to kill him. Why don't you stick around and watch?"

As I walked away, he was ordering a tankard of ale from the bartender.

When you read travel brochures about New York City, they always tell you how wonderful the museums, restaurants and nightlife are.

They never tell you about the strange people, however, and I think they're missing an opportunity. The Big Apple just wouldn't be the same without all those fascinating folks.

Commercial Break? It's Already Broken

I AM A FAN of TV. I watch it whenever I get the time. But I must confess that in recent years I have not enjoyed television programs like I once did.

What I enjoy most these days is the commercials on televison.

If you watch them close enough, I think you will agree with me that they are much funnier than the situation comedies where millions of dollars are spent.

Some of my favorites are the car commercials.

I have never been able to grasp why they think I would buy a new car so the owner of the dealership can win a free trip to Mexico. I'm sure they're nice people, but I frankly don't care if they ever go to Mexico or not.

I've also never been able to understand why car dealers insist on hollering at me through my television or why they will have their children on the commercial. The children usually close by saying in a very sweet voice, "Buy a car from my daddy. He wouldn't tell you wrong."

I hope the little darlings never find out that their daddies would do most anything to sell a car.

The car dealers and their sales techniques have been

adopted in recent years by lawyers and chiropractors.

The chiropractors are pretty much my favorite. They insist on being on camera. There must be an epidemic of egomania among our nation's chiropractors.

My favorite chiropractic commercial shows a man climbing a ladder. Suddenly he grabs his back in obvious pain. The camera cuts away to a lady picking up her baby. She too suddenly grabs her back in pain. The camera then cuts to a shot of the chiropractor. His eyes are glued on the teleprompter, and in a flat, unemotional voice he says, "Hi! My name is Dr. Doddle Whitlock. I can change your life. Why don't you call me at 555-1837 for your free consultation visit? I can help you. That's 555-1837. I can make you taller. That's 555-1837. Car dirty? I'll wash it. That's 555-1837. Is your wife ugly? I can help! That's 555-1837."

I also like the commercials the lawyers make where they say, "Don't forget the adjuster works for the insurance company. I can help you." Sure he can. You can just look at that old boy on TV and tell how sincerely he wants to help you.

I like the commercials about personal products. You know the ones they show every night right at dinner time.

There is a network spot that has been on the air for several years. It opens up with a man standing at a bus stop. It is pouring down rain. The man is soaked to the skin. The camera comes in for a close-up, and the man with rain dripping off the end of his nose looks up into the camera and with all the sincerity he can muster says, "Diarrhea is no fun in the rain."

That doesn't come as any great surprise to me. I know for a fact that diarrhea is no fun in Las Vegas.

Commercial Break? It's Already Broken

There is another commercial that they insist on showing every night at dinner time. The product is called the "Home Pregancy Test."

This company spends hundreds of thousands of dollars every year to advertise its product. That's okay; that's the way the free enterprise system works, and I wouldn't have it any other way.

The thing that strikes me as strange, however, is that the thrust of their ad campaign is not used to tell about their product. The thing they push and even print on the side of the box in big red letters is: "Can be done in the privacy of your own home."

I wonder if their advertising agency thought you were going to a basketball game to do it.

Not all the strange things on TV are contained in the commercials.

I was watching a rerun of *Superman* not long ago. Superman had cornered the bad guy and was slowly walking toward him. The bad guy had a pistol and was blazing away at the man of steel. The bullets, of course, were bouncing off of his chest harmlessly. Superman was smiling and slowly walking toward the bad guy who continued to blaze away with his .38.

After about twenty-five shots, the crook finally ran out of bullets and in a panic threw the gun at Superman. And Superman ducked.

The other shows on television are almost as bad.

Murder She Wrote is a good series, but did you ever stop and realize that every week someone that Jessica knows is murdered? That's about fifty-two people a year. I don't know about you, but that's one lady I would just as soon not be too familiar with.

A few years back *Mannix* was one of the big private-eye series. It was mostly about how Mannix tried to capture bad guys, while the bad guys were busy trying to shoot him, knife him and blow his car up.

Every week he had one narrow escape after another, but somehow he managed to escape death by an eyelash each time.

I recall one episode where Mannix was talking to one bad guy and another crook came up behind him and let him have it with a black jack. He collapsed in a pile on the ground. One bad guy took out his pistol and pointed it at the unconscious form of Mannix. With an evil smile on his face, he slowly cocked the pistol.

The other bad guy, who was obviously the boss, delivered the funniest line I have ever heard. He said, "Not now, we don't have time. Let's take him with us." Then they loaded his unconscious body into the trunk of the car.

I don't know anything about the boss crook, but I think it's safe to assume that he was not an efficiency expert.

Seeing Red In The Soviet Union

WHEN MOST PEOPLE WRITE or talk about the Soviet Union, they make the point early on that they did not like the government but found the people to be friendly and outgoing.

While it's true that I met some wonderful people there, many of whom would qualify as "characters," I would be less than honest if I didn't say that they were in the minority.

Most of the conversations I had started with a wild-eyed Russian screaming, "Nyet! Nyet! Nyet!" Boy, they say that a lot.

When our airplane rolled up to the terminal in Moscow, the first thing we saw were soldiers all around the airplane. They were wearing dull brown uniforms that looked like they had been washed but not pressed.

When we stepped off the airplane, two more soldiers were waiting just outside the ramp leading to the terminal. They were unsmiling and stared like they were looking at a herd of cattle.

Once inside the terminal, another soldier pointed to some stairs. We were walking through a roped-off area, so there was no danger of going anywhere except where they wanted us to go.

I think one of the most startling things I saw in the Soviet Union was the Moscow airport. It was big and looked like any other major airport anywhere in the world, except for one thing — it was empty.

I don't mean it wasn't crowded. I mean except for us, it was empty. No shops, no ticket agents, nothing and nobody.

We got in line to have our passports checked. The soldier who checked them sat inside a closed booth and looked out at us through a smokey glass. He was in full military dress, including hat. He looked to be about nineteen years old and was all business.

I slid my passport to him through a small opening in the glass. He looked at it and then at me. Then he looked back at the passport and then back at me. This mini-extension of the Cold War went on for about five minutes. Just when I was convinced that the young comrade suspected me of being James Bond, he slid my passport back to me and waved me along.

I don't want to misjudge the morale of the Russian soldier, but the entire time we were there I never saw one smile. Maybe they were embarrassed by their uniforms or maybe they had gas, but for a bunch of nineteen year olds, they don't seem to enjoy life much.

It took them one hour and twenty-five minutes to get our luggage off the airplane and onto the carousel. During the wait, I think I discovered why no one was smiling.

I went into the men's room and found that there were no commode seats. I also discovered that there was only one-half roll of toilet paper. To call it paper is to give it the benefit of every doubt. It was more like a cross between burlap and pinebark. That alone is enough to wipe out smiling.

I also think the toilet paper is the reason great ballet dancers are numerous in Russia. When you spend the first ten years of your life walking around on your toes because your rear end is sore, ballet dancing comes naturally.

It took us another hour to get through customs, where we got to meet some more folks with gas or paperburn.

The trip to the hotel was very interesting. Our guide, a matronly Russian of about forty-five, pointed out interesting landmarks along the way. You learn quickly of the horrors the Russian people went through in the Second World War. Monuments are everywhere, and anytime you enter into conversation, the Second World War always seems to come up.

Driving through the streets of Moscow is an interesting experience. There is very little traffic and all the cars look like 1961 Falcons. There are old 1940-vintage buses everywhere. Many of them — I would say about twenty-five percent — have their hoods propped open with a sawed-off broom stick to keep the old engines from overheating in the hot Moscow summers.

We also saw a lot of motorcycles with sidecars, more often than not with a man driving and a woman and child in the sidecar. I was told later that since it was almost impossible for the average worker to afford a car, many people were opting for the motorcycle and sidecar.

It made sense to me, until I thought about those long Russian winters.

I made a little game out of looking for gas stations. I

never was able to find one in Moscow, although later I saw two in Leningrad.

I thought, How can a nation call itself civilized when they can't put a "tiger in your tank" or sell you "gas with guts"? And in Moscow you can't "trust your car to the man who wears a star," 'cause dang near half the folks in Moscow wear a star — a Red Star.

We finally arrived at our hotel, which our guide said was the largest hotel in the world. It had over six thousand rooms.

We were not allowed to get off our bus until our passports were taken up. Then we were given a card that would get us in and out of the hotel. No one was allowed in without a card. Once on our assigned floor, we were to give the card to a woman on duty and she would give us our key.

This bit of foolishness was designed for only one purpose: to know when you're in your room or, what's most important, when you're out of your room . . . in case they decide to search it. (There was evidence that our room was searched rather completely several times.)

Our room was small with twin beds, a black-and-white TV and no air-conditioning. It was clean but very cheaply furnished. The drapes were faded and frayed around the edges. It reminded me of how hotels must have looked in the United States during the 1930's.

On our second day, my wife noticed the wallpaper curling up in a spot near the floor. I got down on my hands and knees to get a closer look and, to my surprise, found that behind the curling wallpaper our hosts had cut a four-inch square out of the sheet rock and lowered a large microphone down between the wall studs. They had then tried to stick the wall-paper back over the hole, but the paste had not done its job and there it was, plain as a pimple on a cheerleader. I thought it was a very clumsy attempt to hear my wife Diane and me talk about military secrets.

While I was still on my hands and knees, Diane said, "What is it?"

"The room is bugged," I said.

She immediately took me in the bathroom, closed the door and started to flush the commode over and over. (A trick she learned to cover our conversation by watching James Bond.)

Between flushes she said, "What are we going to do?"

I said, "If you don't stop flushing that thing, we're going to drown."

She didn't laugh.

I continued, "Look, we don't know anything that the KGB could possibly be interested in. However, since they have gone to so much trouble and expense, I do feel an obligation as a visitor to their country to entertain them while I'm here."

Twice a day, for the rest of our stay in the hotel, I would sit down in a chair very near the microphone and say in my best radio voice, "Blue Leader, Blue Leader, this is Cobra One, Blue Leader. The frost is on the pumpkin."

I would then pause for about three beats and say, "The quick brown fox jumped over the big red dog."

To this day, I don't know for sure if anybody was listening, but I sure hope that I kept their decoding department busy for a little while at least.

Ludlow Porch

THE HUMOR

I doubt that the average Soviet citizen sees a great deal of humor in his lifestyle or in the way his government runs the country. There were, however, many things that I found to be very funny about Mother Russia.

In the hotel in Leningrad, there was a big neon sign in the lobby that proclaimed: "American bar open 24 hours a day. Closed from 12 till 2 for lunch."

They serve a soft drink at almost every meal. The label, of course, is written in Russian so it's impossible to tell what it says. There is, however, a big picture of a pear on the label. This wouldn't be so funny except the drink is banana-flavored.

The women in the Soviet Union do not shave their legs or under their arms. One day in a snack bar, we were sitting one table away from a very attractive young lady who was wearing a sleeveless red dress. She yawned and then stretched with her arms over her head, revealing probably the hairiest armpits behind the Iron Curtain. I turned to my wife and said, "That's the most hair I've seen in one place since a horse fell on me."

The only place in the Soviet Union where the Christian religion is practiced to any extent is in Lithuania. The people line up for blocks to get into church on Sundays.

The people in Lithuania are poor, and therefore the churches are poor. They certainly get no help from a government that wishes they would go out of business.

Lewis Grizzard, who accompanied us on the trip, went to a Baptist service while we were there. Later he was talking about how poor the church was. I knew he was fishing for a straight line, so I gave it to him by asking, "Lewis, how poor *was* that church?"

He said, "The church was so poor that the congregation had to furnish their own snakes."

In a country like Russia where you're told what you can and cannot do, religion is first on the list. You are told not to bring more than one Bible into the country and you must take it with you when you leave. You are also told that no religious literature or tracts can be brought into their country.

The government goes to great lengths to keep religion away from the masses. One day in a store, a Russian man standing beside me sneezed. I said, "God bless you . . . pardon the expression." The man didn't understand me, but both my wife and I got a big laugh out of it.

Most of the stores in the Soviet Union don't have any signs on them. It's really not important because we couldn't have read them if they'd been there.

One day Diane and I decided it would be fun to go to a Russian grocery store. We were really interested in what they had, how they sold it, and what kind of shape it was in.

We tried walking around, looking in store windows for awhile, but that failed to produce any results. We attempted to ask some passers-by about how we could find a grocery store, but we couldn't find anyone who spoke English.

We finally decided that a taxi was the way to go. Once inside the cab, we tried to tell the driver to take us to a grocery store. When all else failed, I said, in very slow syllables, "Gros re store." He gave me a blank stare.

Ludlow Porch

Then I said, "Pigglyski Wigglyski. You savvy? Pigglyski Wigglyski." Nothing. We never found a Russian grocery store.

Ice in Russia seems to be a constant source of consternation for bartenders and waiters. I guess God sends them so much ice in the winter that they have a hard time understanding why anyone would want any in the summer.

When you ask for ice, they become openly irritated. The Russian word for ice is *lewd*, and when you ask for it they look at you as if you had said something lewd.

I did find a formula that seemed to work. If you ask for a drink with ice, you get one piece of ice. If you ask for a drink with a *lot* of ice, you get two pieces. If you want more than that, you give them your cigarette lighter and they bring you a bowl of ice.

Getting ice in your room at the hotel is another problem. They don't have room service and they don't have ice machines. On every floor of the hotel they have an old-fashioned refrigerator with a little bitty freezer at the top. When you want ice, you do down the hall to where the hall monitor sits. You always take a present with you.

As you approach her, you have the bribe in plain sight. I usually carried a blue baseball hat. I would walk up to her desk and say, "Lewd."

She would go to the little bitty refrigerator, open the freezer, and hand me a tray of ice. I would hand her the baseball cap and she would say, "Spahsseebah." I would smile and say, "Fernando Lamas." She would smile and repeat, "Spahsseebah." I would smile again and say, "Delores Del Rio."

I know it's a long shot, but I had this mental picture of her plowing through her Russian/English dictionary trying to find out what "Fernando Lamas" and "Delores Del Rio" meant in Russian.

How can two countries so far apart on the question of ice ever agree on arms control?

One night Lewis Grizzard and I decided it was time to sit down for one of our long-overdue gabfests. My beautiful wife, Diane, Lewis and myself started our evening in a Moscow night spot. We had an adequate meal and sampled every known brand of Russian vodka. Then we changed to champagne. When the hour grew late, we walked across Red Square and headed back to our room at the hotel.

We sat in our room and drank up all the vodka and champagne that we had on hand. We decided that we were still thirsty, but by now it was after midnight and everything was closed. There was a large dining-type area next to my room and there was a big party going on.

Lewis said, "Don't worry. I'll go next door to that party and get us some more champagne."

He left and was gone about thirty minutes. We were starting to be worried about him. After all, there was the matter of the language barrier, plus he had had a great deal to drink and had gone into what was obviously a private party with only Communists attending.

When I was just about to go after him, he knocked on the door.

He was smiling that famous Grizzard drunk smile. Beside him was absolutely the most evil-looking character I had ever seen. The man looked like an Arab. He had jet black, shoulder-length hair and a long handlebar mustache. He had a painted-on smile that he held like an oil painting.

Lewis said, "Luddy, I'd like for you to meet the man who is going to get us some more booze."

I said, "Lewis, this man is obviously a She-ite Muslim. Where did you find him?"

Lewis said, "Oh, no, you must be mistaken. I met him at the party next door. I can't be sure because he doesn't speak English, but I have reason to believe that this lovely fellow is from Beaumont, Texas." Turning back to the man, Lewis said, "Ain't that right, Tex?"

The man just stood there smiling.

I said, "Lewis, how could he be from Texas? He doesn't even speak English."

"Why, hell, don't you know nothin', Ludlow?" he said. "Lots of folks in Texas don't speak English." With this, Lewis turned to the man and said, "You are from Texas, ain't you?"

No reply. Lewis said, "Do you speak English?" No reply. Just more of that painted-on smile.

Lewis turned to me and said, "See, I told you he was from Texas. I'll be right back with the booze."

"I don't think it's a good idea for you to go off alone with Ali Baba there," I said. "He looks to me like he's just waiting to find an airplane to hijack."

"Don't be so damned suspicious, Lud. I told you he was my buddy." Lewis put his arm around his new friend and started off down the hall singing "The eyes of Texas are upon me . . . ."

When they were out of sight, Diane said, "You shouldn't have let him go off alone with that man."

But it was too late then. The longer they were gone,

the more worried I became. In about fifteen minutes, there was a knock on my door. When I opened it, there stood Lewis with a bottle of champagne in each hand.

"Where on earth did you get the champagne?" I asked.

He said, "I ain't sure. I just gave my old buddy Tex sixty dollars and he came up with it."

THE TAXIS

You see a lot of taxis driving around in Moscow, but most of them have only the driver inside.

At first I thought that it was strange to see all those vacant cabs. However, before our visit was over, it became apparent that neither the Russian government nor the taxi drivers want any passengers.

You cannot just hail a passing cab in Russia. It is actually against the law for a cabbie to pick you up at random on the street. We found out from our guide that there were two ways to catch a cab. You could have one pick you up at the hotel, if you were willing and able to call and make reservations twenty-four hours in advance, or you could go wait on the street at a taxi stop and hope one would stop.

We tried the second method several times, only to have empty cabs by the thousands pass us up.

On our second day in the Russian capital, Diane and two friends, Jackie and Margaret, heard about this great restaurant and lounge in another hotel. They decided it would be fun to check it out. They were unaware at the time of the rules and regulations governing the use, or rather non-use, of Soviet taxis.

They walked out of the hotel just as a taxi was

dropping three passengers at the curb. Before the surprised cabbie could react, three crazy Americans piled into his cab. He was terrified. There were policemen and soldiers everywhere, and here were three laughing tourists breaking the law and making him an unwilling accessory.

He started his protest the way most Russians start a conversation—by looking very perplexed and saying in a loud voice, "Nyet, Nyet, Nyet!"

They, of course, didn't know what he was so upset about, but they did know that it was almost impossible to get a taxi in Moscow. They also knew that they had one and that Lenin himself, accompanied by all the demons in hell, was not going to get *their* taxi.

A policeman walking down the street had seen them get into the taxi. He was about a half-block away when he witnessed the illegal act and was running toward the taxi to right this wrong that was being committed against the Communist way of life.

Jackie said to the driver, "You must be illegally parked, because here comes a cop."

He did not understand English, but like cab drivers the world over, he knew that a cop running toward him was not a good thing.

He pulled the gear shift into low and drove away across the giant parking lot with the Russian cop in hot pursuit. He was hunched over the wheel like a drag racer, his three passengers laughing like crazy in the back seat. Traffic stopped in front of him as they left the parking lot and entered the street. The cop was still in pursuit. The cabbie started to blow the horn. The traffic opened up, but the horn stuck and continued to blow in one long, loud blast.

About a block down the road, traffic was stopped at a red light. The cab stopped, horn blaring and passengers giggling. The light seemed to stay red for hours. The other motorists started to hang their heads out of their windows and scream at the cabbie. They were screaming in Russian so the three Americans could not understand, but it was loud, insulting and pretty obvious they were talking about his Mama in Russian.

Diane has one of the greatest senses of humor in the whole world, and once something strikes her funny, she gets hysterical and nothing can stop her laughter. Except time . . . a lot of time.

Sitting in the back seat of the taxi in the middle of Moscow, horn blaring and other motorists screaming, was just more than she could handle. The absurdness of the whole thing hit her like a scene from a Marx Brothers movie.

Her giggles turned into soft laughter as the horn continued to blast and the insults grew louder. Then the soft, lady-like laughter turned into absolute hysterics. It was apparent, almost at once, that the cabbie found Diane's laughter harder to handle than the stuck horn or the screaming motorists.

Margaret and Jackie were busy trying to get the now-guffawing Diane to cool it. But it was too late.

The driver looked back at her several times with hate in his eyes. Diane laughed even louder. Suddenly the driver jumped out of the cab and started around it.

Margaret said, "Dear God, Diane, he's coming to kill you."

Even the prospect of being beaten up by a Russian cab driver could not bring her laughter under control.

They quickly tried to roll the windows up. No luck. They were broken. Diane even tried to get out of the taxi. Same story. The doors were broken and would not open from the inside.

When the furious driver reached the front of the taxi, he stopped and jerked the hood open. He started to pull wires out by the roots. Finally, he found the right wire, pulled it and mercifully the horn stopped blowing.

When they finally reached their destination, the driver charged them about four times what he should have for the ten- or twelve-block ride.

Diane was still whooping as they left the cab driver and walked into the hotel.

Among people who don't smile much, let alone laugh, I suspect that Diane's laughter probably set détente back thirty or forty years.

THE SUBWAYS

Lest anyone get the impression that I didn't like anything about the Soviet Union, let me offer a couple of words about the subways: they're wonderful

The people in the U.S. in charge of our mass-transit systems would be well-advised to copy the city of Moscow's subway system.

To say they are clean is not to do them justice. They are spotless. There is no graffiti. I think their close proximity to Siberia is responsible for that.

The floors and walls are immaculate. In each subway stop you can see several people sweeping and mopping.

The escalators that take you down into the subway

were much steeper than any I had been on before, and they traveled about three times as fast as a stock car.

I asked our guide how deep the subways were under the streets of Moscow. There was a long pause from her and in a stern, school-teacher voice, she said, "Why do you want to know?"

I said, "No reason. I was just curious, because they seem to be much deeper than ours."

Another long pause as she weighed her words. "Our subways are a very important part of our Civil Defense, and any information about them is a state secret." It was obvious from her tone of voice that it was a closed subject and time for me to hush.

THE VETERANS

Everywhere you go in Russia there are reminders of what the people went through in World War II. Monuments are as common as frowns.

The veterans of that war are held in great esteem by everyone. It's easy to spot them because they still wear their military ribbons on their civilian clothes, and in some cases they wear the medals they won. It is not uncommon to see a man wearing twenty-five or thirty medals on his suit coat. They start at the lapels and go all the way down to their waists.

These veterans are held in such high regard that people actually stand up and give them their seats on the bus or subway. In all situations they are loved and respected. The people on the street obviously feel a great debt to these men, and they show it with their respect and love.

Ludlow Porch

This is another area where I feel we could take a lesson from the Russians.

THE TRAIN

I love everything about trains. I have ridden trains anytime I could since I was a child. I like Pullman trains, day trains, club cars and cabooses.

My childhood heroes were the conductor who said, "Booooard," and the wonderful dining-car waiter who said, "Them eggs cooked all right for you, Mr. Porch? If they ain't, you just let me know, and I'll get you somemo'."

I love every train song ever written, from the "Chattanooga Choo-Choo" to "The City of New Orleans."

I would rather ride a train than unwrap a Christmas present.

Therefore, it was good news to me when they told us that our trip across the Soviet Union would include not one but *two* train rides, one of nine hours and one of fourteen hours.

I should have known.

It would be much easier to tell you what the trains in Russia are *not* than what they are:

1. They are *not* air-conditioned.
2. They are *not* equipped with dining cars.
3. They are *not* equipped withh club cars.
4. They are *not* equipped with baggage cars.
5. They are *not* clean.
6. They are *not* fit for hawgs.

Our train car came equipped with a heavy-set, middle-aged woman wearing a dark-colored, ill-fitting uniform, complete with a beret. Her only duties seemed to be to scowl at the passengers. She did serve hot tea once after heating the water on a wood-burning stove.

The compartments on the train were small and not very comfortable. They held four people, and since you slept very close together, it helped if you knew your fellow passengers.

The bathrooms on the trains were so filthy that you knew before you went inside that it was not a place where you wanted to spend a lot of time.

Riding a Russian train will take a lot of the romance out of rail travel.

THE LIES

The Soviet govenment lies about almost everything. It is as much a part of their government as taxes are a part of ours. They do it almost automatically and, for the most part, they do it for no reason.

We were required to go to what they called friend-ship houses; a better word would have been propaganda houses.

They gathered us in large, beautifully decorated rooms where they assured us that we would be given answers to any questions we might have about the Soviet Union.

Before any discussion started, we got a lecture on how peace-loving the Soviets are. It went on and on. Their spokesperson was always glib and lied at the drop of a hat.

Some of the things we were told were:

—"Any Jew who wants to can leave Russia in a moment's notice."

—"You can buy an American newspaper on any street corner."

—"Our press does not write anything bad about the government because there is nothing bad to write."

They told us that anyone could retire at fifty-five years of age.

When I asked why I saw so many men and women sweeping the streets who were in their mid-eighties, the reply was, "Oh, they're just making extra money."

The trip to Russia was very interesting and I learned a lot. I learned that compared to the United States, Mother Russia ain't even in it.

I learned that we shouldn't take things for granted like owning a car or a house or being able to go to a well-stocked store and spend our hard-earned for almost anything we want.

I learned that Russia is not a God-forsaken country. I learned that it is a country that has forsaken God.

The main thing I learned was that despite all their talk about peace and about how much they want to sit down and talk to us, those folks are not our friends. As my old grandmother would have said, "They sure will bear watching."